Women in Wartime
Britain 1939-45

Clive Hardy & Deborah Linton

iNostalgia

Women in Wartime
Britain 1939-45

Birmingham's War Production Workers Week was a major attempt by the city's industry to recruit more women for essential war work. The photograph was taken on Colmore Row. September 1941. (*Birmingham Post & Mail*).

(Opposite page). Stirrup pump at the ready, Mrs Northwood prepares for fire watch duty at the Marlborough Street Labour Exchange, London. March 1944. (*Daily Mirror*)

Clive Hardy & Deborah Linton

Clive Hardy and Deborah Linton have asserted their rights under the Copyright, Designs and Patents Act 1988, to be identified as the authors of this work.

ISBN 978-184547-256-6

Published by iNostalgia, 355 Wilmslow Road, Fallowfield, Manchester. M14 6XU.

Coming to the aid of housewives in Hull. Following air raids, this outsize mobile vacuum cleaner went door-to-door to clear away soot and other debris. July 1943. (*Hull Daily Mail*).

Contents

Introduction

The Second World War heralded new frontiers for British women in public life. From munitions workers to codebreakers, gunner girls to land girls, fashion to football, wartime brought about rapid and vital change, opportunities, employment, and wages. While men were conscripted to fight on the front line, women had new roles to play in education and business, agriculture, and the armed forces.

Born of necessity and circumstance, a country historically fired by manpower was now fuelled by woman power; by wives, mothers and daughters temporarily liberated from the view that their only role was at home and instead relied upon to both raise their children and keep Britain, and the war effort, working.

This book is a celebration of that; a collection of images that recount and commemorate the collective role of women in wartime and explore what it looked and felt like for millions who, during Britain's darkest hour, shone as they fed and fuelled the home front, raised children, and used their brain power to help win the war. Society did not instantly reward them with the equalities in pay and opportunity that they had earned; the fight for that had only just truly begun. But the wars, both First and Second, and the interwar period, brought many 'firsts' for Britain's women who, during those bleak years of bombing and the Blitz, of loss and rationing, used their long overdue independence to further their nation's freedom.

The role of women in the Second World War - which shall be the focus of images compiled in this book - begins with the legacy of the First.

At the outbreak of war, in 1914, the women's suffrage movement - and particularly the campaigns of the suffragette movement spearheaded by the Pankhursts, of Manchester, and their Women's Social and Political Union - had gathered substantial pace. As men were drafted into fight and women called upon in their masses to take on traditionally male roles for the first time, the increasingly militant moves to win women the vote, that were making headlines before the war, were halted and political differences downplayed for a greater good.

The war would, in its own way, help to further the cause though. In 1918, Parliament passed the Representation of the People Act extending suffrage - until that point based on the occupational qualifications of men - to over 8 million women, over the age of 30, who were either householders, the wives of householders, occupiers of property with a £5 annual rent or university graduates. Ten years later, in 1928, this was extended to all women over the age of 21, under the Representation of the People (Equal Franchise) Act, affording them the same voting rights as men.

In November 1918, just ten days after war ended, the Parliament (Qualification of Women) Act was also passed, allowing women to be elected to the House of Commons, another landmark move in their positioning in public policy debate. Nancy Astor, a Conservative, was the first woman to take her seat in parliament, serving from 1919 to the close of the Second World War in 1945.

As the war years played out between 1914 and 1918, the War Office realised that more and more vital jobs could be fulfilled by women.

The Women's Army Auxiliary Corps, later Queen Mary's Army Auxiliary Corps, was established in December 1916 and would eventually see 9,000 women dispatched to non-combat roles in France, freeing up men to fight. The women undertook administrative jobs, answering phones and passing on messages. Those with skills including shorthand or typing could earn higher rates of pay. Others cooked in camps and hospitals. Some repaired motor cars and trucks and built new ones in factories. The women quickly became recognisable from their khaki uniforms and caps. In total, over 57,000 served in it at home and abroad, before it disbanded in 1921.

Women also served in similar auxiliary roles in the Women's Royal Naval Service - or the 'Wrens' - established in November 1917 and the Women's Royal Air Force, established April 1918, fulfilling mechanical and technical roles, cooking, driving and administration. All three services were quickly reformed as the Second World War loomed two decades later.

In rural communities, the Women's Institute was founded in 1915. It was seen as a way of getting women involved in food production as many agricultural labourers were leaving the land to join the armed forces. In February 1916, the Women's Land Army was established, attracting 23,000 recruits to work in agriculture, haymaking or timber cutting. Women made big strides in notable fields too. Before war, there were around 200 female doctors in Britain, but a shortage of trained medics gave rise for more to step into critical roles. Volunteer nurses travelled to France to care for sick and wounded soldiers while others went to battlefields in France and Belgium to drive ambulances. War did not stop breakthroughs either; Marie Curie, the first woman to win a Nobel Prize, invented a mobile X-ray unit, in France, and trained women to operate it, treating Allied soldiers on the battlefields.

Britain also employed its first women police officers - known as the Women's Patrols - while others took on work on the railways in such roles as ticket collectors and porters. They also worked as bus conductors, as tram drivers, in power stations, dye works and laboratories; jobs that were all returned to men when war ended. But it was work in the munitions factories that is often viewed as the most vital and the biggest employer of women in the final year of the war. The female 'munitionettes' put their own lives on the line, working among toxic - and in the case of 200 women, deadly - chemicals to produce bullets and shells.

By the end of the war there were some two million women in traditionally male jobs. With job parity came the - unfulfilled - expectation of pay parity. In the final year of war, bus and train workers went on strike in England and Wales, for the first time demanding equal pay. Their demands were met only with a five-shilling bonus. Like so many other roles, as war ended so did women's work, with the jobs returned to men as they arrived home. The profound change that women had experienced in wartime would not last.

Munitions workers during WWI. March 1918. (*Mirrorpix*).

As war ended, feminist Millicent Fawcett, declared: "The war revolutionised the industrial position of women - it found them serfs and left them free." And yet, despite their wider participation in public life during the war years, in the interwar period women struggled to cut through. Efforts to further female participation in decision-making and policy debate remained stifled and women's issues sat low on the agenda, in poor compensation for their contribution to the war effort. While they had broken free of the perception that their only contribution to the labour market was through domestic service, breaking through glass ceilings and equal opportunities were still decades away.

Dreams of liberation and parity in gender roles and remuneration were quickly silenced as men returned from war and the status quo followed with them. One legacy of the war was trade unions as a place for women - female membership almost tripled by the end of the war making women's issues workplace issues.

By the 1930s around one-third of British women over the age of fifteen worked outside the home. Sisterhood did not always come first, though. Single women, widowed by war, believed their need for work should be prioritised over those with husbands. In 1921, female civil servants passed a resolution, requiring women to leave their jobs when they married, which lasted until the end of the Second World War.

If political and social reform still had catching up to do, it wasn't going to restrain all the ambitions of the modern 1920s and 1930s woman who had enjoyed her taste of personal freedoms. Women expressed themselves through socialising, more public-facing lifestyles, enjoying music, dancing, and fashion. Under wartime and post-war rationing, skirts and hairstyles had gone shorter and restrictive corseted styles had given way to more practical garments and a boyish silhouette; as the twenties turned into the thirties, flapper fashions and jazz, hair dye and Gatsby-style silks heralded the return of glamour before wartime austerity made an unwelcome return.

Worlds apart. Daily Mirror photographer Horace Grant snapped herring girls at Great Yarmouth. The same year, a colleague snapped the latest fashions at Royal Ascot. (*Daily Mirror*).

In 1939, Britain once more found itself darkened by war clouds and, once again, women stepped up. For the second time in a century, Britain needed its housewives to keep cogs in motion both at home and on the home front. 'One million wives wanted for work,' declared Ernest Bevin, the Minister for Labour, as he heralded the arrival of the Essential Work Order, in 1941, which required all women aged 18-50 to register for jobs. Women were categorised in two ways: those considered 'immobile'- women who were married and either pregnant or with children under fourteen at home - were invited to volunteer; 'mobile' ladies - single and married women without dependents - could be sent anywhere in the country to work. By 1943, almost 90 per cent of single women and 80 per cent of married women were working on the land, in factories or in the armed forces. The make-up of Britain changed and the female workforce and auxiliary forces, disbanded after the First World War, were ramped up. While war was no great leveller, a woman's worth was no longer predefined by her place in society - although marital and family status still held too much sway for many - but, again, by circumstance and necessity.

The gradual drafting of women did not begin in 1941, by which point Britain was in full throes of the Blitz, but in the days of 1939 leading up to Neville Chamberlain's declaration of war. With conscription imminent, both the Women's Royal Naval Service (WRNS) and the Women's Auxiliary Air Force (WAAF) of the First World War were reformed, inviting women to take up non-combatant work to support the forces serving on Europe's frontline. Across the two services, women worked first as clerks, kitchen orderlies and weather forecasters, then as mechanics, engineers, electricians, and balloon site operatives, tasked with the heavy work of raising and lowering the enormous barrage balloons that deterred enemy planes. Even the future Queen, the then Princess Elizabeth, trained and served as a mechanic and driver, aged nineteen, proving that status was no barrier to service among Britain's women.

The Women's Land Army, established to farm and feed Britain through the First World War, was also swiftly re-established. The 'land girls' in their tan dungarees and hair turbans became poster girls

Telephonists at the Whitley Bay Exchange try out their gas masks during an ARP exercise on 22 August 1938. These masks differed from the standard adult type, having a built-in microphone that could be plugged into the switchboard. (*Newcastle Chronicle & Journal*).

for the women's war effort, with thousands from towns and cities dispatched to arable land for as little as £1.8s (£1.40) for a 56-hour week. By 1944, 80,000 women were farming rural Britain. Among them were 6,000 'lumber Jills', the affectionate name given to female members of the Timber Corps, who took on the heavy load of forestry.

Women were once again relied upon to keep the country's buses, road and rail networks moving. In London alone, 20,000 female workers took on jobs in the city's transport companies and the double-breasted navy coats, caps and messenger bags of bus conductresses became a common feature of the capital during wartime. On the railways, what began as unskilled roles expanded to everything from signalling, locomotive fitters, and electricians. It is estimated that during the war, around 60,000 roles previously the reserve of men and boys recruited women and girls to fill vacancies. However, at the war's end, the vast majority once more became a male preserve.

Women took to the skies too. One in eight pilots with the Air Transport Auxiliary were female, shuttling thousands of aircraft from manufacturers to military airfields and carrying out air ambulance work. In total, 165 women pilots served alongside their male counterparts, even winning equal pay from 1943 - a small victory. It was not without sacrifice though; fifteen female pilots lost their lives, most famously, Amy Johnson, who had been the first woman to fly solo from the UK to Australia.

Back on land, some of the best paid, but most arduous, work was to be found in the munitions factories where 950,000 munitionettes or 'canary girls' - so-called because of the toxic, yellow stains left by the TNT they handled - were to be found making bullets and shells. This was dangerous work, involving explosives and heavy machinery, and, just as in the First World War, explosions were a common occurrence and too-often fatal, costing women their lives or their health.

By accident, rather than design, women signed up to the Home Guard (or 'Dad's Army') despite, as the nickname suggests, females never being part of the plan. By the end of 1942, some 50,000 were in support roles and, the following year, the establishment of the Women's Home Defence Corps (WHDC) saw more than 200 units of women drivers, clerks, telephone operators, messengers, and cooks, among other jobs, release more men for combat. Ladies also volunteered for the Women's Voluntary Service (WVS), fostering a major role in the evacuation of more than 1.5 million people, mostly children, from cities, under threat of bombing, to relative safety in the countryside.

Operation Pied Piper, to mobilise children to safe lodgings, was launched in the first days of wartime and saw women of the WVS play a key operational part, ensuring youngsters were correctly billeted out of danger zones and collected at the other end. These same women distributed clothes to the needy and set up mobile canteens, feeding firefighters and wardens, during The Blitz years. The work of the WVS did not end with the surrender of the Axis powers as rationing remained in place. In 1952 Queen Elizabeth II became patron.

The transition into practical roles and the reduced availability of fabrics came with a new utilitarian approach to women's dressing. Fashion would change overnight. With little warning, clothes rationing began in June 1941 as part of the 'war on waste'. Sixty-six coupons were to last one year: a woman's coat took 14, a dress took 11, a skirt, seven, and a pair of knickers, three. A year later, embroidery or appliqué, lace or decoration on underwear and nightdresses was banned. Fashion, the ultimate extension, and expression of a woman's personality became functional, as tax-efficient dressing took over and practical triumphed over pretty. Jumpsuits, nylon stockings, shorter skirts and trousers never went away.

One wonderful, if unintentional, step change of both World Wars was the advent of women's sport. With men away and the Football League on pause, ladies took up the mantle - and loved it - filling football grounds with fixtures between local factory and servicewomen teams and raising money for war charities at the turnstiles.

With many entertainment venues closed, the Second World War delivered a resurgence to women's football, which had been relegated to local recreation grounds, following a ban in 1921 on using grounds belonging to clubs that were members of the Football Association.

Cricket and rugby were popular too and served to remind Britain of the untapped sporting prowess of its women, who'd have to wait another 25 years for the establishment of a women's Football Association.

And what of women's responsibilities as mothers? Before 1939, childcare provision was of little consideration to politicians, given that mothers were expected to stay at home. However, the evacuation of hundreds of thousands of children freed them for war work; others, although exempt by virtue of having young children at home, were keen to contribute too. In 1940, the government recognised day nurseries were needed if they were to get women working in the numbers required to sustain the war effort; childcare provision was expanded, the following year, after pressure from female trade unionists.

While every role that women played, and sacrifice they made, in wartime Britain is to be celebrated, perhaps one of the most exceptional was saved till last. Throughout the war, more than 640,000 women served in the armed forces. This time, though, as war progressed, female members of a Special Operations Executive (SOE) were deemed capable of being trained for combat and even to kill the enemy and, in December 1941, unmarried women aged 20-30 and childless widows became liable for conscription.

Among the WRNS and the WAAFs were plenty of highly efficient wireless telegraphists, women with exceptional language skills and others with the capacity to solve complex puzzles and cryptic crosswords. Some 8,000 of these women, including the country's most intelligent female cryptanalysts, mathematicians, and linguists, found themselves part of a team of codebreakers at Bletchley Park whose work intercepting enemy codes would, eventually, help win the war for Britain.

With VE Day, in 1945, came celebrations - for victory, for freedom, for the men who returned alive to hold their wives and children again and to reclaim the jobs that a female workforce had held for them during their years away at war. The women who saw out and powered the war effort from home, who raised babies, who risked their lives in factories and kept Britain fed and moving, were now surplus to requirement in the workplace. Their battle for recognition and equality may have faced its biggest test - and passed with flying colours - but, in reality, it had only just begun.

Deborah Linton

200+ images in this book are from *Mirrorpix*, Life in Pictures 1903 – today, the syndication and licensing service of Reach plc. The archive contains an estimated 200 million images from Reach plc national and regional titles, and there is a programme to make as many of these images as possible available online. Images are available to members of the public. Please visit the website for further details.

Acknowledgments

This book would not have been possible without the help of the following people, many alas no longer with us. Hilde Marshall, Katheen Pearcey, Shirley Anderson, Bill Greig, Charlie Ley, E Effner, Valpy Street, Freddie Reed, Bernard Alfieri, Freddie Cole, Teddy Baxter, Malcolm Race, George Greenwell, Walter Melbrook, John Heddon, George Edward Malindine, George Roper, Ada England, Joan Nisciel, May Redman, Edith Emily Duff, Betty Hardy, Ada Walker, Cissy Stevenson, Bishop Marshall, Bill Sissons, Truus Taminio, Reg Lowndes, Gladys Merrifield, Warwick Brown, Horace Grant, Jim Facey, Andrew Flint.

ARP (Civil Defence)

The establishment of Air Raid Precautions (ARP) arose out of Cabinet approval in 1935 for the spending of £100,000 (approx. £7,272,956 in 2020) on planning for the contingency of war. It was believed that in the event of war being declared, the aerial bombardment of towns and cities would start within hours, if not minutes. A direct result of the Munich Crisis was a massive surge in ARP recruitment so that by the end of 1938 around 1.4 million people had signed up.

Most ARP members were wardens, whose job would entail enforcing the blackout and then using their local knowledge, access the extent and type of damage so the Control Centre could despatch the appropriate rescue services. The warden was also responsible for getting survivors to a shelter or Rest Centre. The Senior Warden was recommended to make a large informative map of his or her area. Some of the information to be included was the locations of factories, garages, hotels, schools, and cinemas. Also, first aid posts, pharmacies, doctors, police stations, fire watch posts, and hand firefighting equipment. All water supplies including fire hydrants, emergency water tanks, canals, streams, rivers, ponds. All places where a member of the public could take shelter in the event of a raid. The map was to be hung up in the Wardens Post, and, if possible, a copy given to each warden. There were normally six wardens to a post, and one post for every 500 people. More than 90 per cent of wardens were part-timers, and one in six was a woman.

The Control Centre was responsible for directing First Aid Parties and Rescue Men. First Aid Parties consisted of four men, an ambulance, and a driver. All were experienced first aid workers having been trained by either the Red Cross, St John's Ambulance, or the St Andrew's Society. Their main task was to assist the Rescue Men in releasing trapped casualties and then administer what aid they could. A decision would then be made as to whether a casualty needed further treatment at a First Aid Post or hospital. First Aid Posts (FAP) were usually manned by a trained doctor, a trained nurse and nursing auxiliaries. There was normally one FAP to every 15,000 people.

The threat of gas attack was taken seriously and ARP drills in which gas masks had to be donned became regular occurrences. In certain circumstances householders were advised to select a room, basement, or dry cellar for converting into an airtight, gas-proof and splinter-proof refuge room. The most important ARP work was preventative as in evacuation and the use of shelters.

Special duties were devolved to the police, special constables, and the Police War Reserve, including control of air raid warning systems, liaison with the military, billeting of soldiers, preparation of military routes, piloting of army convoys through towns and cities, photographing prisoners of war, anti-invasion preparations and security duties.

The Women's Voluntary Service for Civil Defence was formed in 1938 as a branch of ARP, its initial function to inform households on how to protect themselves and their community in the event of air raids. There were no ranks. The WVS was divided into twelve Regions conforming to the same geographic areas as the Civil Defence Corps. Members made bandages, swabs, and hospital clothing in large quantities. Others staffed mobile canteens and emergency field kitchens. During November 1940, the WVS launched a major recruiting campaign for staffing Rest Centres. The take up exceeded expectations, Sheffield alone enrolling 1600 recruits by the beginning of December.

The ARP organisation also embraced the fire services. In the 1930s, though many towns and cities possessed highly professional fire brigades, they could not be expected to answer all the emergencies resulting from a major air raid. The answer was the Auxiliary Fire Service (AFS). Because of the situation in Europe, the Fire Brigades Act, 1938, allowed regular brigades to increase their establishment of men and appliances, and recruiting began for the AFS.

AFS equipment usually consisted of trailer pumps towed behind suitable vehicles. The pumps came in a variety of sizes capable of delivering between 120 gallons (545.5 litres) and 900 gallons (4091.4 litres) of water per minute. Pumps were either single axle, the power to pump the water supplied by a four-cylinder petrol engine, or a four-wheel type with the power supplied by a Ford V8 engine. The wheelbarrow pump was the smallest. It required just one person to manoeuvre it and was designed to be operated in confined spaces.

In August 1939, all AFS and regular units were issued with steel helmets and respirators. The Home Office announced that weekly rates of pay for full-time personnel would be £3 (£200 in 2020) for men, £2 for women (£134 in 2020), and £1 5s (£84 in 2020) for youths aged 17-18 years. Youths aged 16-17 years were paid £1 (£67 in 2020).

Though female members of the AFS received some firefighter training, they were usually kept out of the front line. However, they performed vital duties at fire stations and often went out during raids as crew members of Mobile District Control vans.

Another raid function they performed was taking drinking water to firefighters, often while the bombs were still falling.

On 1 September 1939, local authorities were instructed to put their air raid warning systems on full alert. All part-time AFS personnel were ordered to report to their stations and newspapers published a police notice to the effect that no light from 'a house, office, factory or anywhere else' was to be observable from outside. All illuminated advertising signs and external lights were to be extinguished. There were exceptions such as railway signals. Lights on vehicles and roads must also be dimmed.

It did not always go to plan. There are instances where householders in remote areas of mid Wales and on the Yorkshire moors, blacked out only those windows likely to be seen by a warden. No thought was given that to the fact that the Luftwaffe might see the other side of the building.

Central Birmingham 1 September 1939. Workers at the C&A store busy themselves filling sandbags. (*Birmingham Post & Mail*).

The very latest in blackout fashion accessories – white armlets and waist bands. The Men's Wear Council also recommended men to wear light coloured clothes. The Daily Mirror persuaded several ladies to try the armbands. One said, "People stared at me through the dark, so I knew at once they could be seen and that the experiment was successful. When I crossed the road at pedestrian crossings oncoming cars pulled up at once. The night before, when I wasn't wearing the bands, I had to jump out of the way every time I crossed the road."

One of the more unusual blackout precautions was the daubing of wild New Forest ponies with whitewash so they would be visible drivers on the forest roads. (*Daily Mirror*).

(Opposite page). A volunteer messenger and her Rudge motorcycle combo working for the Auxiliary Fire Service, Birmingham, 6 September 1939. (*Birmingham Post & Mail*).

A Gas Identification Squad rehearses the correct way to put on a gasmask. Unit members were qualified chemists, whose job was to identify the various types of gas which might be dropped by the enemy – tear gases, blister gases, lung irritants, and so on. 19 September 1939. (*Daily Mirror*)

ARP exercise, Liverpool. The air raid warden is wearing a new type of gas hood, though as with the baby's respirator it relies upon air being pumped by hand. There were many reports of babies becomin drowsy and this is thought to have been due to an insufficient air supply. All the respirators were fitted with filters manufactured from 80% carded wool and 20% asbestos. (Marsh. *Liverpool Echo*).

HERE THE MONEY GOES

To give you some idea of what happens to money you give to the Red Cross and St. John, now this table:

1ᴰ	buys a small bandage	
3ᴰ	buys a cover for a hot-water bottle	
5ᴰ	buys a slab of chocolate for a convalescent casualty	
/-	buys enough wool for a working party to make a pair of gloves	
6	buys 200 cigarettes for a prisoner of war	
5/-	buys pyjamas for a bombed-out child	

Red Cross needs £10,000 a day at the present rate nding. Please give a little extra for your flag on

D CROSS & ST. JOHN
FLAG DAY—JUNE 5

Members of a Birmingham ARP First Aid Party at the Central Car Park Depot. Full time male ARP staff on what was called 'stand by' worked a 72-hour week (six 12-hour shifts), and female staff worked a 48-hour week. This image is dated 23 April 1940, and the end of the following June there were at least 50,000 women employed full-time on ARP work. (*Birmingham Post & Mail*).

(Below). The Princess Royal (the future Queen Elizabeth II) visits the Red Cross Auxiliary Hospital, Ash House, Etwall, Derbyshire. March 1941. (*Derby Telegraph*).

Fiction meets fact. Warden Percy Dale assisting a victim of the blitz. However, the image of Percy and his ward was a studio pose for the Civil Defence recruitment poster above. However, the background in the above photograph is very real. It was taken in Paternoster Row by *Daily Mirror* photographer George Greenwell on 29 December 1940. ARP was officially rebranded Civil Defence in 1941, though both names continued to be used. By 1944, Civil Defence full-time strength stood at 66,900 of which 10,000 were women with 799,400 men and 179,800 women registered as part-time volunteers. (*Daily Mirror*).

(Opposite page). Published on the front page of the *Daily Mirror* on Thursday 17 October 1940 under the banner headline I WON'T LET THEM HURT YOU. The photograph shows warden Mrs Mary Couchman protecting her young son and two of his friends from shrapnel and debris. According to the story, Mrs Couchman was taking a cigarette break in the wardens' post in small the Kentish village where she lived, when the sirens sounded.
Seeing her son Brian, aged four, playing some distance away, she ran out of the post. As she did, the bombs began to fall. She gathered Brian and his friends Johnnie Lusher, aged four, and Gladys Ashsmith, aged seven, into her arms and huddled over them, protecting them with her own body.
According to the story, a *Daily Mirror* photographer happened to be in the village when the incident occurred. When the raid was over, he told Mrs Couchman, "You are a brave woman." Her reply was, "Oh, it was nothing. Somebody had to look after the children."
The photographer was none other than George Greenwell. When George took this image has been the subject of many a debate. It carries a file date of 16 October, and its publication is significant because the previous Sunday had seen extensive day and night activity by the Luftwaffe over a wide area of the UK. During a raid on London on the Sunday night, the Coronation Avenue block of flats at Stoke Newington, had been demolished by a bomb that penetrated five floors before detonating. The basement had been designated Public Shelter No.5 and many people were present when the flats collapsed on top of them. There was worse to come when survivors discovered the basement flooding with water and sewerage from ruptured pipes and the air was running out.
Despite the best efforts of the rescue services the scene quickly moved from one of rescue to one of recovery. It took more than a week to recover the 154 dead of whom 128 were eventually identified. Other casualties for London that night was a further 175 people killed with 458 injured, whilst elsewhere in the UK casualties amounted to 33 killed, 68 seriously injured and 83 slightly injured. Additionally, 25 people had been killed and 108 injured in a daylight attack on the capital.
As with the Percy Dale image, Mrs Couchman served as a boost to morale in difficult times. (George Greenwell, *Daily Mirror*).

The Air Raid Shelter signs denote that P&O House, Cockspur Street, Manchester, has been designated for use by members of the public in the event of an air raid. Before the outbreak of war, local authorities were ordered to survey and refurbish existing vaults, cellars, etc, for use as public shelters in town centres. (*Manchester Evening News*).

(Opposite top). Named in honour of Sir John Anderson, the Anderson shelter was a familiar sight at the bottom of many a garden and thousands of examples still survive eighty years after the start of the Blitz. By the end of October 1939, approximately 2,250,000 Andersons had been distributed free of charge, but a change in Government policy resulted in those earning more than £5 a week (£334 in 2020) having to buy their own at prices ranging from £6.14s (£6.70p) to £10.18s (£10.90).

Andersons consisted of corrugated steel sections with a curved roof bolted to sturdy rails to give the structure strength. Andersons proved to be robust, surviving almost anything save a direct hit. Ideally, the shelter was 'planted' three feet into the ground, the remaining exposed sides and top then covered with compacted earth at least eighteen inches thick. Some, as pictured here, added a sandbag blast wall in front of the entrance.

Depending upon ground conditions, it was found that during the winter months Andersons could become waterlogged. This made their use more than a little unpleasant and during raids some householders preferred to take their chance staying in their homes rather than being up to their knees in muddy water. Even so, Andersons proved to be robust and survive anything save a direct hit. At least three million Andersons were built. (*Bristol Post*).

(Opposite bottom). The Morrison shelter was designed specifically for use in the home by those who had neither a garden nor a backyard. Named after Home Secretary and Minister of Home Security Herbert Morrison, this new type of shelter looked like a table.

The carcass measuring 6 ft 6 ins (length) x 4 ft (width) x 2 ft 6 ins (height) or 1970 mm x 1270 mm x 745 mm, was made of steel fitted with wire mesh sides. It could be assembled by two people in a couple of hours and had to be installed on the lowest floor of the house. There was enough room for two adults and depending on their size, one or two children. And yes, many used them as kitchen tables.

Once again, they proved robust, with occupants surviving the collapse of two and three storey houses. By the end of the war at least one million Morrisons had been issued. (Official. *Daily Mirror*).

Bedding down for the night in one of London's deep shelters. These were in addition to the London underground stations. (*Mirrorpix*).

(Opposite page top). An emergency cooking centre at work. Manned by the WVS and volunteers, they provided those bombed out of their homes with hot meals. (*Newcastle Chronicle & Journal*).

(Opposite page bottom). Rehearsal to test the effectiveness of a newly established rest centre at Cherry Tree Hill School, Derby. The air raid warden is on tea duty. July 1941. (*Derby Telegraph*).

In the Tuesday 2 December edition of the *Daily Mirror*, Sister Clare's column was devoted to influenza. 'Influenza is in the air this month, and it is passed from person to person. That's how you catch it.' Our image shows nurses dosing out medicine for the prevention of flu at St John's tube station. December 1941. (*Daily Mirror*).

All female AFS crew on pump and hose drill, Glasgow, December 1941. (*Daily Mirror*).

(Opposite page top left) A Salford City Police WPC on her rounds delivering a refreshing cuppa to officers on traffic duty. To comply with ARP blackout regulations, the police car had had the bulb that illuminated its radiator-mounted Wolseley badge removed. February 1942. (Andrew Flint, *Mirrorpix*).

(Opposite page top right) A WPC on duty at Piccadilly Circus, London. May 1944. A major difference between this WPC and a woman police officer serving during World War One, was powers of arrest. They had been granted to WPCs in 1923. (Charlie Ley, *Daily Mirror*).

The usherettes at the Odeon Leicester Square formed the cinema's firefighting unit. Here they take to the catwalk high up over Leicester Square. February 1943. (*Daily Mirror*).

(Left) Normally a woman ought to feel safe when a policeman was about. However, this War Reserve policeman is John Reginald Halliday Christie, who by the time he resigned from the force in 1943 had already murdered at least one woman. His victim was 21-year-old munitions worker and enthusiastic amateur prostitute Ruth Fuerst. Christie picked her up in a snack bar in Ladbroke Grove and after sex at his home he strangled her with a length of rope. Shortly afterwards Christie resigned from the force and secured an office job at a radio factory in Acton. There he met Muriel Amelia Eady. Muriel suffered from bronchitis and claiming he could offer her a cure, invited her to his flat. Christie had rigged an elaborate piece of kit – a jar containing a liquid. Also, there was a rubber pipe inserted into the top of the jar. The liquid was Friar's Balsam. The pipe was connected to the household gas supply. The Balsam concealed the noxious smell of the gas, which in the 1940s contained carbon monoxide. Once Muriel was unconscious, Christie raped, then strangled her.

Christie would get his just desserts. A short drop and a quick stop on the gallows at Pentonville on 15 July 1953. By then however, he had killed at least eight women including his wife, Ethel. (*Daily Mirror*).

Operation Pied Piper

During the early months of 1939, parents up and down the country received a letter from their local education authority advising them that they were in an area deemed at risk from bombing in the event of war. The letter confirmed that plans were being drawn up to evacuate children to places of safety, though no indication was given as to where those places of safety where located.

"Under the arrangements which are being made the children will gather at the primary school nearest their homes and the older and younger members of each family will as far as possible be evacuated together. They will go to the chosen places in the care of teachers who will remain with them. They will live in the country in houses where they will be welcome. Arrangements will be made to let you know their new addresses as quickly as possible. Children under school age will also be allowed to go if the mother or a woman friend went with them, and all the children of one family will be sent to the same place."

As the international situation deteriorated during late summer, some schools took matters into their own hands. St Chad's Roman Catholic Boys School left Birmingham by train on Saturday 26 August, the day all schools in designated evacuation areas had been ordered to reopen to prepare for a nationwide rehearsal the following Monday. Meetings were held at every school to advise parents and children of what to expect during the rehearsals.

Though the Monday was only a rehearsal, plans were in place that should it prove necessary, the exercise could quickly be turned into the real evacuation. All school children who were at home were to be at their appropriate assembly school by 9.00am. Mothers with children under the age of five were also invited to take part.

Each child should, if possible, bring with them the articles required should the actual evacuation take place. A warm coat or mackintosh, night clothes, a change of underwear and a change of stockings or socks, house shoes or rubber shoes, toothbrush, comb, towel, bar of soap and a face cloth. They should also bring enough food for the day, a tin cup, plate, and their gasmask in its box.

Each child was to wear an identity label listing the child's name, date of birth, home address, name of school attended and destination. There was to be one adult, usually a teacher, for every ten children. Adults travelling on the trains would wear a white armband, usually sporting the initials of the relevant education authority. Should the rehearsal become the real thing, teachers fortunate enough to own cars would go by road to their allotted reception areas. The reasoning behind this was that a school might well be dispersed in groups across several villages, and the cars would come in hand, keeping the groups in contact with one another.

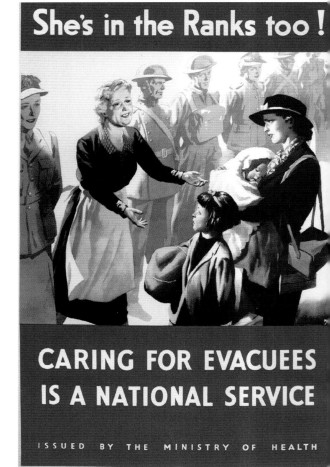

She's in the Ranks too!

CARING FOR EVACUEES
IS A NATIONAL SERVICE

ISSUED BY THE MINISTRY OF HEALTH

Among the designated evacuation areas were the London boroughs, Rochester, Southampton, Chatham, Gosport, Coventry, Birmingham, Derby, Nottingham, Liverpool, Birkenhead, Manchester, Salford, Hull, Grimsby, Bradford, Leeds, Rotherham, and Sheffield. In the northeast and Scotland; Newcastle-upon-Tyne, Gateshead, Edinburgh, Glasgow, Clydebank, Dundee, and Rosyth.

On 31 August, special messengers advised schools that the real evacuations would commence the next day, Friday 1 September, and continue through the weekend or longer where required, regardless of the international situation. Some towns such as Grimsby did not receive the final go-ahead until late afternoon, early evening, by which time the shops were closed, leaving parents unable to obtain clothing and other lastminute items. Making sure the message got home, Birmingham deployed loud-speaker vans to tour the suburbs.

Originally, some local authorities had put forward their own schemes. Sheffield's local educational authority had proposed sending its evacuees to neighbouring and familiar areas such as the villages of north Derbyshire. The Government in its infinite wisdom knew better, advising the Sheffield Emergency Committee in April 1939 that 30,200 places had been secured in Leicestershire and a further 30,100 in Nottinghamshire.

At Sheffield, the London & North Eastern Railway laid on twenty special trains to a variety of destinations including Newark, Bingham, Ruddington, Loughborough and Melton Mowbray. Many of the trains carried only a third of the children expected. The second evacuation train from Sheffield Victoria to Newark had places for 840 children but carried only 266. By the end of the day only fifteen per cent of those registered had left Sheffield.

Mrs Rixon, wife of the headmaster of St Michael's School, Buckingham Palace Road, Pimlico, makes sure the Wheeler children, Patricia, Maureen, Teddy, and Peggy, have all their belongings, prior to the school evacuating. September 1939. (*Daily Mirror*).

It was a similar story elsewhere. The London boroughs saw fewer than half of the 400,000 registered children leave, and in Birmingham only one-third bothered to turn up for evacuation. Manchester was the only large city that could declare the evacuation a success. Its well-organised scheme resulted in 75 per cent of its children leaving the city for places of safety. In Scotland, around 170,000 children and mothers were evacuated to the comparative safety of the country and west coast seaside towns.

Nationwide, between 31 August and 8 September, more than 1.5 million people were evacuated to safe areas. The figure comprised 827,000 children, 524,000 mothers and young children, 13,000 expectant mothers, 7000 handicapped people and 103,000 teachers and helpers. Even these figures, impressive as they are and considering that not one serious or fatal accident occurred, was far fewer than the Government had hoped for.

Where the children finished being billeted was anyone's guess. Though taking in an evacuee was voluntary, billeting officers were given compulsory powers and could force a household to take evacuees. Households were paid 10s 6d (52.5p but equal to £33.42p in 2020) a week for each unaccompanied child they took in and 8s 6d (42.5p equal to £26.72 in 2020) a week for each child and mother. Some slum children finished up in the homes of the wealthy while some children from wealthy families ended up living in slums. One of the better-known stories involved a mother and her young child from a Glasgow tenement. Billeted with a well-to-do family in the countryside, all was going well until the toddler squatted down in the middle of the room to defecate on an expensive Persian carpet. Seeing the look of horror on her host's face the mother was quick to admonish the child with the words, "Don't do it on the nice lady's carpet. Go and do it in the corner like at home."

Mothers and toddlers await their evacuation train at Percy Main railway station. 7 September 1939. (*Newcastle Chronicle & Journal*).

The use of toilets was not the only problem. Many of the children were infested with lice. As the evacuation programme had commenced at the start of the new school year, most schools had had insufficient time to organise their annual après summer holidays delousing parades.

At a meeting of the Newcastle and Gateshead Band of Hope Union, Lady Trevelyan stated she was shocked to hear a story concerning an evacuated child in the south of England who, when on arrival at his billet, and asked if he would like some biscuits replied, "Biscuits? What I want is beer and chips. That's what I get at home."

The lack of bombing soon resulted in children and expectant mums in the nearer reception areas drifting back home. As early as 29 September 1939, officials at Coventry estimated that 800 children had returned to the city. On 16 November 1939, Robert Barbour, Town Clerk at Hawick,

reported to the Town Council that of the 1120 evacuees that had come to the town, only 383 remained. Similarly, despite the efforts of local authorities to disuade them, the majority of expectant mums evacuated from London to Wiltshire, had returned home. On 24 November 1939, Councillor W E Wheeldon, told a meeting of the Birmingham Education Committee that a thousand evacuated children a week were returning to the city. The Government refused to pay the return fares of those voluntarily leaving the reception areas.

However, the fall of France, the bombing of towns and cities, as well as the V1 and V2 attacks, would all result in further evacuations, though they would be more local affairs.

Evacuees, and their helper, who is sporting a white armband initialled LCC for the London County Council education authority, at Salehurst or Robertsbridge in East Sussex. The image carries a file date of 3 September 1939. (*Daily Mirror*).

The Home Front

Sunday 3 September 1939 saw a flurry of emergency regulations and precautionary measures put in place. As well as the immediate closure of all places of entertainment and sports fixtures likely to attract large crowds, people were expected to keep off the streets unless it was necessary for them to be out.

The Board of Trade immediately banned the import of all goods that could be supplied by UK-based manufacturers. The first list, released on 4 September included, pottery and glassware, cutlery, textiles, clothing, footwear, clocks and watches, toiletries, perfume, makeup, luxury foodstuffs, toys and games, musical instruments, motorcars, certain listed chemicals, paints, and office equipment.

Also announced was the rationing of petrol from 16 September. Petroleum distributors were to pool all supplies and only one grade would be supplied to the public. It was to be called 'Pool' motor spirit and sold at the fixed price of 1. 6d (7.5p) a gallon (4.54 litres). The ex-pump price of 'Pool' was fixed for at least fourteen days, and garages were free to sell off their remaining stocks of individual brands of petrol. An announcement would be made on 4 September as to applying for petrol ration books.

Anyone owning gold coins or foreign exchange was required to take it to the bank and sell it to the Treasury. Currencies already listed included: US dollars, French francs, Swiss francs, Guilders, Swedish crowns, and Argentinian pesos. Businesses requiring gold and foreign exchange to meet contracts made before the declaration of war had to apply through their bankers. It now illegal to export gold, banknotes, or foreign currency. Later in the war, the actor Noel Coward was convicted of racketeering and fined £1600 (£81,378 in 2020) for failing to register his US dollars with the Treasury.

On 29 September 1939, every household in the UK was required to write down the details of every man, woman and child living at their address. Name, sex, date of birth, occupation, address, marital status, and where relevant, membership of the armed forces, auxiliary forces, civil defence, and reserves. The information was collected by officials on 30th and 31st and was used in the issuing of identification cards.

At first, the ID card for adults had a buff cover, a child's ID card a manila one. During 1943 a blue cover ID card began to be issued. Interestingly, the only type of civilian ID card to carry a photograph of the person, was the green card issued to certain government employees. ID cards had to be presented upon demand or at a police station within 48 hours of the request to see it being made.

Just four days after the declaration of war, petrol ration books were issued for the first time and by the beginning of November the Government was warning garages that forged petrol coupons were already in circulation. Of course, there were ways of circumventing petrol rationing. One, simply drive off without paying, and two, steal the stuff from the armed forces. This latter activity was proving so popular that by May 1940 military fuel was dyed and the police were mounting random checks on the contents of civilian petrol tanks.

The Fuel & Lighting Order also came into effect on 7 September, its aim to reduce the total quarterly consumption of electricity to 75 per cent of the amount used in the quarter ending 30 June 1939. Twelve days later it was announced that coal rationing would start on 1 October. Householders were required to register with a licensed coal merchant and would then be advised by a local official as to their basic quantity entitlement each quarter.

In January 1940, sugar, bacon, and butter went on ration. However, as many working-class families could not afford butter and could rarely afford streaky bacon, which according to the J Sainsbury archive were 1s 3d (6.5p) and 1s 6d (7.5p) per pound respectively, stockpiles soon built up and the Government decreed double rations at no additional cost for everyone. For those unable to afford butter, margarine made from whale oil with added vitamins was available at 6d (2.5p) per pound.

The weekly ration allowance per person was two ounces (56.7 grams) of tea (none for the under-fives), two ounces each of butter, sweets, and fats, four ounces (113 grams) each of margarine and sugar. Extra cheese was issued to workers with no canteen facilities and a special ration was organised for vegetarians, though they were forced to surrender their meat coupons. Prime cuts of meat were rationed at six ounces (170 grams) per person per day, though people were free to buy quantities of cheaper cuts up to the cash value of six ounces of prime beef, mutton, or pork. Horsemeat was available and not subject to rationing.

1940 also saw the introduction of a points system of rationing on tinned meats. Tinned crab, salmon, oranges, pineapple, lemons and so on were not officially rationed because they were almost impossible to get hold of. The Government thought they had solved the fish crisis by importing 11 million tins of South African Snoek, a relative of the tuna. Despite a flood of Snoek recipes, the majority of those unfortunate enough to acquire a can, complained that it was smelly and inedible. After the war, so many cans were left unsold that the stuff was relabelled and sold as cat food.

Under the Defence Regulations, it was illegal for shopkeepers to sell rationed goods without coupons. Shopkeepers were deliberately targeted by the Food Office which sent undercover operatives into shops with the sole intention of persuading the shopkeeper to part with a rationed item without receiving the appropriate coupon in exchange. The operatives were at liberty to try any hard luck story they cared to produce and to persevere until the shopkeeper either handed over

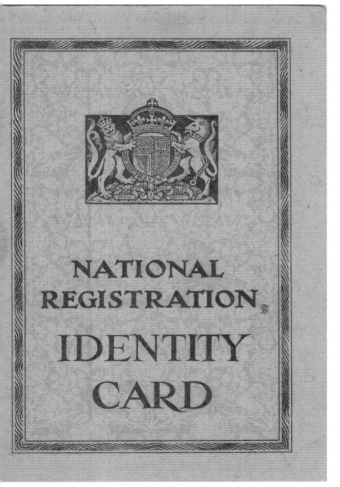

Mrs Prince moved between Gloucester, Nuneaton, and Bristol to be with her husband who was in the RAF. (Collection Clive Hardy).

the goods or refused point blank. Any shopkeeper falling for the hard luck story was then prosecuted under the regulations. As it was a strict liability offence, the shopkeeper was guilty as charged.

Shopkeepers and traders took the used coupons they had collected to the Post Office where they were exchanged for a voucher. The voucher could then be set against their next wholesale purchase. The regulations required that the used coupons be returned to the appropriate issuing office where they would be checked. This soon proved unworkable. Millions and millions of coupons were soon sloshing around the country and whatever the security was, it was not fit for purpose. The Ministry of Food kept up the pretence that every coupon was checked whereas in reality, it was a very small percentage. It did not take long for the underworld and unscrupulous shopkeepers to catch on that there was no way the ministry could check every coupon. The Post Office, responsible for collection and shipment of coupons had been overwhelmed in a matter of days and immediately modified the system so it could cope by refusing to check or count coupons handed in. Shopkeepers and traders could take in their bundles of coupons which they simply signed for. The unscrupulous shopkeeper got his all-important voucher, in return, the ministry got a bundle of coupon sized newspaper clippings or blank paper bearing a bogus name and address.

Other targets for the Food Office were cafes and restaurants. Under the regulations it was a strict liability offence to serve a customer more than two courses, though it was not illegal for a customer to pay for their two-course meal, leave the restaurant, then come back in, sit at a different table and order two more, possibly different courses. The meal-snooper's task was to persuade staff into serving them a larger meal than permitted. Not only was the restaurant automatically guilty, so too was the poor waiter or waitress who was charged with 'aiding and abetting.'

Bureaucratic eccentricity reached new heights when it was decreed that bread could no longer be served in cafes and restaurants at lunchtime.

Notices appeared in all seriousness in the Press announcing the fact that Food Office officials would be mounting lightning raids on eating establishments to see what diners had on their side plates. It was completely barmy as bread was never rationed during the war.

The British Restaurants established during the war appear not to have attracted too much attention from the Food Office as they had set menus, guaranteeing the customer a decent meal for a set price.

One way of supplementing official rations was by growing your own. Allotments sprang up everywhere from school playing fields to railway embankments, even the dry moat at the Tower of London was turned over to growing vegetables.

In July 1940, the *Nottingham Evening Post* was advising its readers to pay a visit to the Estates Department at the Guildhall, where an advisory bureau on gardens and allotments was being established. Land was being made available and the council were willing to come along and plough it. Council tenants, nearly all of whom had decent sized gardens were encouraged to grow vegetables to the extent of digging up flower beds and lawns.

RATIONING BEGINS TODAY !

"O.K., Nasty—But You'll Pay!"

Being able to grow your own took on an importance all its own when then Acquisition of Food (Excessive Quantities) Order came into force. Officials were given powers to enter homes and inspect the contents of the larder. If there was more than a week's ration, even by a small amount, the householder faced prosecution that could result in a fine and possible imprisonment. Before the war, housewives who kept a well-stocked larder were applauded. Now they were hoarders. Mrs Elsie Carter, of Caversham was fined £36. 15s (£2103.84p in 2020) for hoarding. Mind you, the contents of Elsie's larder were a little on the excessive side. 75 pounds (34.02 kg) of preserves; 98 tins of mixed fruit; 82 tins of milk; 81 tins of meat, and 196 tins of fish.

During June 1941, tomatoes seemed to vanish from the shops. At the beginning of the month, they were on sale at an average price of 2s. 6d (12.5p) per pound, so few people were disposed to parting with their hard-earned cash. By the third week in June, they had become subject to a control maximum retail price of 1s. 2d (6p) per pound and flew off the shelves.

Before the war, tomatoes were imported in vast quantities from the Channel Islands and the Netherlands. Now, the country relied on home-grown produce and the crop was at least three weeks late due to frosts during May. They would be available in July, though not enough to satisfy demand.

In mid-August 1940, the Government banned the manufacture of hosiery it classed as "luxury trade." On 21 October, Nottingham's largest firm of silk throwsters, Windley & Co, closed with

The evacuation of the British Expeditionary Force from the beaches of Dunkirk resulted in troop trains departing Dover at the rate of one every eight minutes. Troops were fed and watered along the way, their trains stopping at stations where volunteers (especially members of the WVS) were to hand armed with tea, beer, buns, and sandwiches. (Official. *Western Mail*).

the immediate loss of 400 jobs. The Government insisted that only Government contracts could be worked on and Windley's did not have any. What they did have was enough silk to manufacture 2.5 million pairs of stockings. Along with other manufacturers they sought permission to release 1.5 million pairs of stockings for the Christmas 1940 market. They were refused and ordered to export them, only they did not have an export market.

Worse was to come. Without almost any warning clothes rationing was introduced in June 1941. The announcement was timed to coincide with a Bank Holiday thereby enabling the Board of Trade to advice retailers before they reopened. Everyone was given 66 coupons to last one year, and the same number of coupons had to be surrendered whether a garment was bespoke or off the peg. A woman's coat took fourteen coupons, a frock took 11, whilst a skirt was seven coupons, and a pair of knickers took three.

As clothes rationing was introduced before everyone had received a clothes ration book. An interim measure allowed people to buy cloth, clothes, footwear and knitting wool using a surplus page of margarine coupons in their food ration books. Each coupon counted as one coupon toward the purchase of clothing or footwear.

The Board of Trade fixed the maximum prices for all clothing, household textiles, bedding and cloth both within the Utility range and outside it as well as for utility boots and shoes. Clothing for children under the age of four was exempt as was wool and silk thread for mending, sewing thread, and boot and shoelaces.

In February 1942, Sir Stafford Cripps told the Commons that "personal extravagance must be eliminated altogether." No petrol for pleasure motoring, a cut in the clothing ration and sporting events curtailed. Cigarettes were not officially rationed though many tobacconists looked after their regular customers first.

October 1939 and ration books are being prepared for distribution. Each book had a black market value of £5 (£334.22p in 2020), and unmarked books became a prime target for burglars. The biggest haul was 100,000 pristine books taken from the Food Office at Romford. (*Newcastle Chronicle & Journal*).

Silk stockings became a thing of the past and women resorted to painting their legs with gravy browning and drawing a black line with a pencil to represent the seam. Others used makeup. Both methods worked reasonably well unless it rained. Then the 'stockings' often turned into a confusion of gravy browning splodges and leg flesh. In 1938 more than 33 million pairs of stockings were imported but by 1944 it had dropped to 718,000 pairs, not including those that might be had from American bases.

From 1 June 1942, restrictions were placed upon women's and girl's underwear and nightdresses. No longer were they to be supplied with any form of embroidery or applique, or similar decoration, and lace of any type was banned. The order affected nightdresses, pyjamas, slips (petticoats), knickers, cami-knickers, vests, and all garments not completed by 1 June.

On Monday, 4 December 1944, the *Daily Mirror* published a piece from one of their correspondents on the latest wheeze to beat the Board of Trade and at the same time save on clothing coupons. Around the north and midlands there was a growing demand for reels of coloured thread, the stuff used for fancy needlework. However, the reels, usually costing 3s 2d (16p) for four, were being used for something else – to make stockings, and there were plenty of ladies around willing to knit them for 2s 10p) to 2s 6d (12.5p) a pair. The stockings were not fully-fashioned, but the thread was flexible enough for them to fit as well as stockings costing three times as much.

On I June 1944, the Government began issuing more than 45 million new ration books. Before anyone could get their new book, they had to ensure their ID card and present ration book were in order. The ID had to be signed with the holder's signature (see page 29), and all information was correct. Page 36 of the present ration book had to have the names and addresses of the person's usual retailers either written or stamped in the spaces provided. Provisions were made for those people who might have difficulty getting along to pick up their new book. All the books for a household

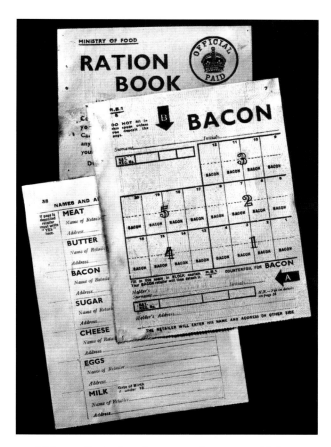

could be collected at the same time, even if the surnames were different.

That same month at Airdrie Sheriff's Court, housewife Jean Johnstone was fined £5 (£226.75p in 2020), with the option of thirty days imprisonment, for using a delay in the transfer of her family's registrations to uplift rations from two grocers. From one, she used her husband's and three daughters' ration books to obtain 2 pounds of sugar, 12 ounces of cheese, 24 ounces of fats and one pound of preserves a week for seventeen weeks. From the other, she used her own book to obtain 8 ounces of sugar, 3 ounces of cheese, 6 ounces of fats and half an ounce of preserves.

Registering for food rationing, Birmingham Town Hall, 21 November 1939. (*Birmingham Post & Mail*).

An unwritten rule was "If you see a queue, join it!" This queue outside Birds Confectioners, St James Street, Derby, set the then record for its length. Then again, the word was out that cakes and pastries were available. (*Derby Telegraph*).

Romford Co-op. At least the dividend of 1s 4d in the pound would have put smiles on faces. (*Mirrorpix*).

The points system for canned goods came into force on 1 December 1941. Top grade tinned salmon, if it could be found, was rated at 16 points (a month's worth of points for one person), though three months later it had risen to 32 points. (*Birmingham Post & Mail*).

War-Time COOKERY
to save fuel and food value

Issued in the National Food Campaign Exhibition
1940

LEWIS'S   MANCHESTER

People were actively encouraged to invite Allied service personnel to their homes. The American armed forces were firm favourites given their rations were far more generous than our own. February 1944. (*Mirrorpix*).

(Below). Potato Week. Members of the public look over the numerous potato-based dishes on display at the Electricity showroom, Derby. 4 March 1942. (*Derby Telegraph*).

Go through your wardrobe

Make-do and Mend

Fashions for the Anderson shelter? Siren suits were sale at Lewis's, Birmingham, at the beginning of October 1939. They were one-piece garments made from fine woollen fabric, with a buttoned bodice, and well-cut trousers, available in navy, green and brown, sizes 38, 40 and 42 hips. A snip at 29s 9d. Other styles available included a bed quilt come wrap, and a coat with attached hood. (*Birmingham Post & Mail*).

When clothes rationing was introduced, every man, woman, and child was issued with an appropriate ration book containing pages of coloured coupons, yellow, olive and magenta. Only one colour could be used at a time, the idea being to stop people using all their coupons in one go. The annual allocation was 66 coupons for an adult (later reduced to 48) and 70 for a child (to allow for growth).

When buying an item, such as man's coat, jacket, or blazer, the customer handed over 13 coupons together with the money to pay for it. Even so, the allocation wasn't generous, and clothing was often recycled. Adult clothing reworked to make dresses, frocks, and blouses for children. The WVS stepped up to the plate, running garment exchanges. (*Daily Mirror*).

(Opposite page top). One piece of good news announced in the *Daily Mirror* on Saturday 25 July 1942, was the imminent abolition of purchase tax on utility clothing. Utility dresses were made from cloth of specified fabrics sold at fixed prices. The tax cuts meant a woman's coat costing £4.4s (£4.20p) would be reduced to £4, and a costume costing £3.14s (£3.70p) would see a reduction of 3s 3d, whilst 3d would be knocked off a pair of artificial silk stockings. Cotton print would be reduced by nearly 8d a yard.

On 18 July 1942, Binns Fashion was advertising ladies' dresses in artificial silk and Rayon at prices ranging between 31s 5d (£1.52p) and 55s 9d (£2.79p), with skirts priced between 14s 5d (72p) and 19s 8d (97.5p).

Mrs Jeannie Adamson, MP for Dartford, made the front page of the *Daily Record* after attending the Commons in a Utility dress. It was black, with a neat panel at the back, ending with two pleats. It had a bolero effect in front and was cambroidered. As Hugh Dalton declared. "Utility clothing doesn't mean uniform rigid standardisation." (*Daily Mirror*).

(Opposite page bottom). The shape of things to come. During September 1944, Spooner & Co, Plymouth's largest department store, held its first fashion parade since its premises were destroyed during the blitz of 21/22 March 1941. Among those modelling the latest fashions were three sisters. Kay Wilshaw, aged 17, in the wedding dress, and behind her are her sisters Phyllis and Eileen.

Spooners were up and running by the beginning of 1942, though until the early 1950s its departments were scattered across various locations around the city. The company moved to new premises in Royal Parade during 1954-56. (*Mirrorpix*).

Smiles all round as the first of six pairs of knickers are made from an old night dress. 1941. (*Mirrorpix*).

A Glasgow tram masquerading as a large carboard box was one of the city's attempts at persuading people to save wastepaper and cardboard for recycling. (*Daily Record*). In Derby a housewife bundles up newspapers for salvage. The recycling of newspapers as well as old clothing, was well established in the UK long before the start of the war. (*Derby Telegraph*).

The residents of Temple Green, Gateshead, clear their homes of surplus items made of metal. The hunt for salvage metal included ripping up the tracks of abandoned tramway systems and ripping out ornate metal railing from cemeteries, municipal parks, and from the walls outside people's homes. (*Newcastle Chronicle & Journal*).

Keeping the Nation Fed

In 1939, most farms were mixed farms of between 50 and 250 acres and although marketing boards existed and the price of wheat guaranteed, the industry was still depressed. Out of 29 million acres of arable land, seventeen million acres was permanent grassland.

The coming of war would forever change the face of British farming. Under the supervision of the County War Agricultural Executive Committees, farmers were paid a subsidy of £2 (£133.69p in 2020) an acre to plough up grassland for crops. By the end of the war, nearly six million acres of what had been permanent grassland was under cultivation, some of it thanks to government financial assistant for drainage works and reclamation projects.

Farming became increasingly mechanised. At the outbreak of war, around 56,000 tractors were in use on UK farms, and by its end the number had risen to 203,000. Efficient use was made of combined harvesters, which were moved from farm to farm as they were needed. Between 1942 and 1945, the number of disc harrows in use more than doubled. There was also a massive increase in the use of fertilisers.

One lesser-known function of the County War Agricultural Committee was to assess and classify farms according to productivity. Upon receiving a classification, a farmer could apply for assistance – usually in the form of WLA personnel, as well as equipment. Subsequently, if a farmer failed to comply with directives, he could in the worst-case scenario be evicted. The most famous, and the most tragic case, involved a Hampshire farmer who was ordered off his farm for failing to comply with a directive to plough four acres. The man refused to leave, and the police were called. Barricading himself in the farmhouse, the farmer opened fire with a sporting gun wounding several officers. The police retaliated with tear gas but when that failed, armed reinforcements were sent for. They stormed the building shooting the farmer dead.

In 1939 the UK produced 4.26 million tons of grains, increasing to 7.74 million tons in 1943. Over the same period, production of potatoes rose from 4.35 million tons to 8.54 million tons, whilst meat fell from 1.18 million tons to 754,000 tons. Imports of sugar fell by two-thirds, wheat by a third, and butter by around 70 per cent.

The Women's Land Army (WLA) was reformed, having been disbanded at the end of World War One. A sizeable minority were from the countryside, though the bulk of them were from towns and cities. After a few weeks training, the WLA recruit was allocated to a farm. The work was hard, the hours were long, and the pay in the early years of the war was just £1.8s (£1.40p) for new recruits for up to 56 hours a week. The volunteers were, from December 1941, joined by conscripts.

The war on waste is the subject of this photograph from May 1941. Mrs. Worthless is caught red handed throwing all and sundry into the dustbin. Bread, potato peelings and other kitchen waste. The message was, "Many brave lives and boats have been lost bringing this food to you. Utilise this scrap now and save lives." (*Mirrorpix*).

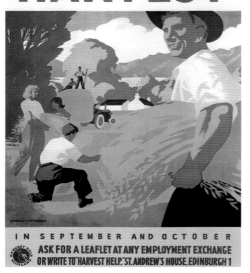

A day out in Reading for the WLA. In 1943 WLA conditions of employment were improved with a pay rise and the granting of one week's holiday a year. (Valpy Street. *Reading Post*). (Below). Members of the WLA harvesting oats. August 1941. Members of the public were encouraged to spend their holidays, as well as earning some extra money, picking crops such as potatoes, peas, and cauliflower. (*Mirrorpix*).

Members of the National Fire Service turned a blitzed area around Red Cross Street Fire Station into an allotment. They levelled the debris then covered it with soil brought in from Hampstead and Finsbury Square. The view is looking toward Aldersgate Street. July 1942. (*Daily Mirror*).

A blitzed wing at Guys hospital was levelled at turned into an allotment for the use of nurses and staff. August 1943. Factories also got in on the act. The Ford Merlin engine plant at Trafford Park, Manchester, took over sixteen acres of land adjacent to the site and used it to grow vegetables for the work's canteen. (*Mirrorpix*).

The Smedley's Cannery at Wisbech working to full capacity in October 1943 as locally grown fruit and vegetables are bottled. (How, *Daily Mirror*).

A queue for horse flesh. Off ration meat included whale and horseflesh as well as rabbit, hare, pigeon, blackbirds and so on. Though horseflesh was lean like venison, many people balked at the idea of eating it whereas they had no qualms about beef, mutton, or pork. The government even published pamphlets such as on how to cook horseflesh, and how to pluck, draw and cook pigeon. There was plenty of horseflesh to go around and it was supplied to zoos to feed their big cats, though it first had to be marked with green dye. (*Daily Mirror*).

Hop pickers at Paddock Wood station having just arrived by train from London. For much of the twentieth century, hop picking was a popular summer job for tens of thousands of Londoners. The basic hopper hut was around 9ft (2.74m) by 10ft (3.04m), usually made of timber, though some were brick, and during the 1930s they were being constructed out of breeze blocks. Floors were of beaten earth, water was normally supplied by standpipe and toilet facilities were of the earth closet variety, though there were always exceptions. Hop pickers were responsible for supplying their own furniture, though the growers usually supplied straw for filling mattresses. (*Daily Mirror*).

At least the hop pickers know where baby is. Paddock Wood. (*Daily Mirror*).

(Above). Herring ready for smoking. January 1940. (Right) Fish from North Shields arrives at Billingsgate. (Below). Early morning scene at Manchester fish market as housewives rush to buy surplus fish. November 1944. (*Mirrorpix*).

Hawker employees Winnie and Dolly Bennett were usually to be found building Hurricane fighters. However, despite working ten hours a day, six days a week, they still found the stamina to follow their love of ballet. This image is of them giving a performance in the works theatre, along with another showing them working on an aircraft, appeared on page 7 of the *Sunday Mirror*, 3 January 1943. (*Mirrorpix*).

Entertainment, Leisure and Sport

Immediately following Neville Chamberlain's broadcast on Sunday 3 September 1939, the Government announced the immediate closure of all places of entertainment as well as all indoor and outdoor sports gatherings. The closure was to last until further notice. It was a precautionary measure aimed at reducing casualties in the event of air raids. The measure would be kept under review with the possibility that some cinemas and theatres might be able to reopen in some areas should events allow it.

Even so, Denham Studios soon had the country's first war film in production. Starring Ralph Richardson and Merle Oberon, *The Lion Has Wings* was in cinemas before there had been any air raids. It was produced by Alexander Korda, a good friend of Winston Churchill. Korda promised to have a feature length propaganda film on general release within one month of the declaration of war. The movie relied on cobbled together stock film as well as some location filming at RAF bases at Hornchurch and Mildenhall.

When places of entertainment reopened, patrons were to be refused admission if they were not carrying the gas masks. A cinema manager in Newcastle upon Tyne claimed that after performances his cinema was littered with impromptu 'containers' holding half bricks and wastepaper, the punters having abandoned their 'respirators.'

Going away on holiday would become but a memory as restrictions were placed on the use of petrol for private motoring and coach excursions. Also, people were actively discouraged from making unnecessary train journeys and with areas of coastline now off limits to civilians, Holidays at Home became the thing. People could still travel, though it might well be limited to local bus services, and the LMS did run excursion trains from Nottingham to the gardens at Sutton Bonington, a round trip of about twenty miles.

Belle Vue, Manchester, played a pivotal role in Manchester's 'Holidays at Home' campaign. It was one of only a handful of venues of this type allowed to remain open even though the war proved to be a challenging time as restrictions impacted heavily on its activities. Crowd pulling events such as the firework displays were cancelled and some of the fairground rides mothballed. The Christmas Circus continued though it was restricted to afternoon performances only. After the Manchester Free Trade Hall was destroyed by bombing, the Kings' Hall at Belle Vue became the home of the Halle Orchestra.

Belle Vue Zoo became a refuge for animals evacuated from zoos forced to close. Unfortunately, those species reliant on food supplies from overseas suffered through lack of availability and subsequently many died. Belle Vue's penguin population was wiped out through lack of fish and the sea lions developed stomach ulcers from consuming beef soaked in cod liver oil. Also, the entire collection of tropical fish died when the heating system failed due to a disruption in the gas supplies. The monkeys lived on boiled potatoes, and the lions were fed horse meat, though the regulations required it to be marked with a harmless green dye.

One direct casualty of the bombing was a bull bison killed by splinters from an anti-aircraft shell. Splinters from anti-aircraft rounds also damaged the Reptile House, and keepers were armed with rifles as a precaution to prevent animals escaping should the zoo be hit by bombs.

Many animals have hearing more acute than humans and keepers reported that they showed signs of distress during air raids even when the raids were many miles away.

The UK's leading spectator sports of the 1930s were association football and greyhound racing. Introduced from the USA in 1926, greyhound racing was an instant hit with the working class as they too could own and race dogs. It proved popular enough for many tracks to hold four meetings a week. When the September 1939 restriction was eased, the tracks were each limited to one afternoon meeting a week.

During the winter months, a razor blade, a bottle of Indian ink, a pen, and a steady hand, was all a felon needed to work the greyhound track Tote scam. The Tote was reduced to using glorified raffle tickets, and, if the winning number was a 3,6,8, or 9, it was easy enough to scratch off the offending portion and alter a 3 to an 8, or an 8 to 3 and so on. The Tote clerks often had little chance of spotting a fake as ARP regulations meant they worked under subdued lighting. Tracks soon became associated with spivs and dodgy deals and were frequently raided by joint military and civil police looking for deserters. Punters were rounded up and ID checks carried out.

The war also witnessed a resurgence of women's cricket, and association football. Even a few rugby union teams were formed. Many were factory teams, though the fire service and women's services also formed sides. Because of petrol shortages fixtures tended to be at a very local level.

With the men away at the war, women's association football had been the great spectator sport of the 1914-18 war, with top sides such as the Dick, Kerr & Co works team, and St Helen's Ladies, not only playing quality football, but capable of attracting capacity gates at Football League grounds. The bulk of the gate money went to war charities. Any post-war chance of establishing women's League football was killed off in 1921 when, out of jealousy at the popularity of the women's game, the Football Association banned them from using member's grounds. Women's teams were reduced to using local authority recreation grounds.

After the second world war, the Football Association's bigoted attitude was still there for all to see. In 1947, the Kent FA suspended a referee simply because he was the manager/trainer of Kent Ladies FC. In 1921 the FA had relied on spurious opinion from a couple of Harley Street quacks that playing football reduced women's fertility. The Kent FA's ruling was that "women's football brings the game into disrepute."

Though the Jockey Club would not licence women to ride in races, they could own horses. Dorothy Paget, daughter of Lord Queensborough

was a leading National Hunt owner. Her horse *Golden Miller* won the Cheltenham Gold Cup five years running as well as the 1934 Grand National. Another of her horses, *Insurana*, won the Champion Hurdle in 1932 and 1933. Her horses continued winning during the war.

In 1943 a Pony Derby was run at Epsom as part of Epsom and Ewell's Wings for Victory Week. Seven top jockeys took part including Steve Donoghue and Gordon Richards. The race was won by E Smith on *Stand at Ease*. The horse was owned by the Reverend Mother Veronica.

On a lighter note, 1 September 1939, was the day 21-year-old Miss Marguerite Wilson, a professional cyclist with Hercules Cycle & Motor Co, set a new record for the 'End-to-End' the 870-mile run between Land's End and John o' Groats. She completed the route in two days, 22 hours, and 52 minutes, beating the previous record set in 1938 by Lilian Dredge of three days, 20 hours, and 54 minutes.

The production line for the mass market Philco 'People's Radio' at the Philco Radio & Television Corporation factory, Perivale, Middlesex. Costs were kept down by using moulded Bakerlite for the cabinet. By September 1939, it is thought nine out of ten homes in the UK had a wireless. (Edward George Malindine, *Daily Herald*).

Tommy Handley stands in a line up described at the time as 'modern girl secretaries' at the premier of Jack Hylton's new review *ITMA* (*It's That Man Again*). Following the success of four pilot shows, *ITMA* was chosen as the ideal format for lampooning the war and the Nazi leadership. Each programme was a send-up of Radio Luxembourg, which had ceased transmitting at the outbreak of hostilities.

ITMA was given a regular slot and repeated for the benefit of British forces overseas. Popular with listeners from all levels of society, Jack Train is supposed to have been told by a gentleman of the royal household that 'If the war were to end between 8.30-9.00pm on a Thursday night, none of the Household would dare tell the King until *ITMA* had finished.' (*Mirrorpix*).

(Right) The country's highest-paid entertainer and top box office star George Formby, entertains Londoners sheltering in Aldwych tube station on 10 November 1940. (*Daily Mirror*).

FEBRUARY

DEFYING FEBRUARY'S
SNOW,
JANE TOILS UNTIL SHE'S
ALL AGLOW,
TO LOSE HER LABOUR
WITH A KISS —
THERE'S "SNOWMAN" WHO'D
NOT MELT AT THIS!

Mrs Laura Henderson, owner of the *Windmill Theatre* with the *Revudebelles*, the ladies who appeared in the theatre's famous, or infamous, nude tableaux vivants. The theatre ran continuous performances from 2.30pm till 11pm. During the war, the *Windmill* proudly boasted "We Never Closed," though others would argue that "We Never Clothed" was more to the point. Apart from the compulsory closure of all places of entertainment between 4-16 September 1939, the Windmill's claim is correct – even at the height of the London blitz.

The theatre was also home to the *Windmill Steeplechase*, the name given to the chaos at the end of each performance when the patrons at the back of the theatre rushed forward to occupy seats vacated nearer the stage. (George Greenwell. *Daily Mirror*).

Drawn by Norman Pett, the *Jane's Journal* strip cartoon featured regularly throughout the war in the *Daily Mirror*. Whatever the storyline, Jane somehow managed to lose most of her clothing. It has been claimed that following copies of the newspaper featuring a fully naked Jane arriving in North Africa, the British 8th Army advanced five miles. Winston Churchill claimed the Jane cartoon was a morale-booster and the British war effort's secret weapon. (*Daily Mirror*).

Rest and relaxation for WAAFs in the form of a life drawing class. December 1940. (*Mirrorpix*).

The 14-strong *Moon & Stars* Concert Party was comprised of former professional artistes who were serving with AA units. Sitting at the table are Bombardier Denis Fowell and Gunner Henry Sprake. Next to Sprake is Margaret Chester and sitting almost in front of her is her sister Nora. The cast are dressed for a gypsy routine. Central Hall, Derby, December 1940. (*Derby Telegraph*).

Vera Lynn entertains service personnel. Known as the "Forces Sweetheart" Lynn's enduring songs include *We'll Meet Again*, *There'll Always Be an England* (which sold 200,000 copies of sheet music between September and November 1939), *A Nightingale Sang in Berkley Square*, and (*There'll Be Bluebirds Over*) *The White Cliffs of Dover*. She also toured the Middle East, India, and Burma with ENSA. (*Sunday Mirror*).

(Opposite page top). The ATS band was formed in 1941 under Junior Commander Angela Stebbing's leadership. It started as an eighteen strong drum and bugle band which soon proved popular, performing at parades throughout the UK. A dance band was also formed, and it featured regularly on the BBC. The band's HQ eventually moved to Gower Street, London, and in January 1944 the unit was awarded full military band status, its strength raised to fifty-five. A pipe band was also added. The band ceased to exist in 1946 as its members were demobbed. (*Mirrorpix*).

(Opposite page bottom). As night fell on Saturday 8 March 1941, London was subjected to a major attack. Being underground, the *Café de Paris* was considered, and advertised, as the safest restaurant in town and attracted a well-heeled clientele. The resident musicians were Ken 'Snakehips' Johnson's 12-piece Caribbean jazz band. The 26-year-old Johnson was one the leading black British musicians of the day, having broadcast on radio and made appearances on the BBC's fledgling TV channel.

Johnson had just begun the second chorus of *Oh, Johnny, Oh Johnny, How You Can Love*, when two bombs smashed down into the basement. One exploded just in front and to the right of the band, decapitating Johnson and killing his saxophonist Dave 'Baba' Williams. The other failed to detonate but split apart, scattering shrapnel around the café. In all 34 people were killed and 80 injured, some seriously. (*Daily Mirror*).

Actress, dancer, singer and musician Frances Day at the Odeon, Kingston, 2 October 1940. Born in the USA, she made her London stage debut in a cabaret double act with John Mills. She was popular during the 1930s, appearing in twelve movies, six stage plays and releasing twenty-two songs. Her only film release in 1940 was the comedy *Room for Two*. During the war Day toured, putting on shows for troops including going to Burma. (Bernard Alfieri, *Daily Mirror*).

The Fairey Aviation football team was drawn from workers at the company's Heaton Chapel Works as well as the test facility at Ringway Aerodrome (now Manchester Airport). Due to travel restrictions, the team played against WAAF and ATS teams around the Manchester area. (*Mirrorpix*).

Paddington station is crowded as thousands attempt to get away to the coast for the 1941 August bank holiday weekend. Visitors were banned from those resorts inside the military defence zone, such as Southend, Margate, Ramsgate, and Brighton. Holidaymakers chancing their luck by car were turned back at military police roadblocks.

Winston Churchill was annoyed that seaside coach firms did a roaring trade offering full and half-day 'See the Countryside' trips, squandering fuel that merchant seamen had risked their lives to bring to Britain. As restrictions on the use of petrol for pleasure began to bite, along with the active discouragement of people making unnecessary journeys by train, 'Holidays at Home' became the new normal, with local authorities encouraging events and activities. Excursions by train or bus were sometimes available, but they appear to have been limited to round journeys no greater than thirty miles.. (*Mirrorpix*).

Clocking On

The war was only two weeks old when the government announced the gradual drafting of at least one million women into war work, replacing men called up for service in the armed forces. The plan envisaged they would replace men in unskilled occupations such as bus conductors, railway cleaners, textile workers, clerks, shop assistants, and processed food operatives. An estimated half a million women would also be needed in the munitions industries, though again the idea of training them to undertake skilled work was not being actively considered. However, the French Government took a different line. There, women were effectively told to stick to women's work, nursing, office, retail, and staying at home raising their children and running their households.

Between September 1940 and the end of 1941, the armed forces and Civil Defence proposed to increase their establishments by a total of 1,750,000 men and 84,000 women, a course of action that would require 500,000 workers giving up their jobs. Over the same period, the munitions industries were looking to recruit an additional 1,500,000 people. It was proposed that women should be recruited to fill as many unskilled or semi-skilled jobs as possible. Single woman in the 19-24 age group were called up.

In March 1941, Minister of Labour, Ernest Bevin, brought in the Essential Work Order, requiring all women aged 18-50 to register for work in one of two categories. 'Immobile' women were married and either pregnant or had children under the age of fourteen living with them. The category also included women whose husbands were serving in the armed forces or the Merchant Navy. Women in this category could not be forced to do war work though they were welcome to volunteer.

The 'mobile' category included single women and married women with no dependents. A Woman with no dependents whose husband was either in the armed forces, Merchant Navy, or living at home, could be directed into work anywhere in the country. Not all women were happy with Bevin's EWO and for good reasons.

The big raids on Germany continue. British war plants share with the R.A.F. credit for these giant operations.

THE ATTACK BEGINS IN THE FACTORY

WOMEN OF BRITAIN
COME INTO THE FACTORIES
ASK AT ANY EMPLOYMENT EXCHANGE FOR ADVICE AND FULL DETAILS

During the TUC Conference held the following September in Edinburgh, H C Kershaw, Colne Valley Weavers Association said, "My personal opinion is that the main reason women will not go into the workshops is that the principal of equal pay for equal work is definitely missing in the war industries." Kershaw pointed out that women sent from Scotland and Wales on EWOs, were receiving only £1.18s (£1.90p) a week of which £1.10s (£1.50p) went on their lodgings, whilst Kershaw himself was on £3.0.6d a week for doing the exact same work. Mrs H Godley of the Guild of Insurance Officials alleged that women wanting to volunteer for the armed forces were being told not to expect their jobs back at the end of the war.

The National Service (Number 2) Act, December 1941, allowed for the conscription of all single or widowed women aged 19 – 30. Conscripts were given the options of working in industry, on the land, or joining one of the women's services of the armed forces. The scheme was quickly extended to include women aged 18-51.

Once registered, a person was invited for an interview at their local Labour Exchange, and, if not already in a job considered essential to the war effort, they would be asked to consider taking up work of national importance. Those refusing could be compelled.

Cissy Stevenson had one of the more unusual jobs. Her husband worked for Coles Cranes, delivering new lorry-mounted mobile cranes to customers and authorities around the UK. With his co-driver called up for military service, Cissy took over as driver's mate. During the blackout, Cissy would often be perched on top of the forward-facing crane jib guiding her husband along darkened streets. One night she was in position as her husband had to drive through the centre of Manchester. She was not up there long. Within minutes of entering the city the sirens sounded and the bombs began falling. It was the start of Manchester's Christmas Blitz.

On 22 October 1939, the Ford Motor Co was asked to locate, equip, and manage a shadow factory for the mass production of Rolls-Royce Merlin XX aero engines. Ford's expertise at mass production was urgently required, though it was also vitally important that aero engine components should be

fully interchangeable regardless of manufacturer. Initially, part of the old Ford factory at Trafford Park, Manchester, was turned into a tool room, and machine tools, technicians and draughtsmen were transferred from Dagenham. Rolls-Royce provided drawings and seconded skilled engineers. By September 1940, several buildings had been erected at Eccles and 2300 workers hired.

As most skilled workers in the UK were already employed, Ford had to rely on untrained men, youths, and women. Even so, the first production Merlins were delivered to aircraft manufacturers during June 1941. In March 1942, Eccles was asked to increase production from 400 to 600 engines a month and by April 1944 the workforce of 17,307 including 5828 women were turning out 900 engines a month as well as a steady supply of spare parts. Mass production at Eccles brought the book price of a Merlin down from £5640 to £2484 each.

Helping with the Christmas mail at the GPO sorting office, Midland Road, Derby, 1939. (*Derby Telegraph*).

As with the Great War, among the jobs soon opened to women was that of bus conductor. By January 1940, many corporation and tramway departments were actively advertising for women to take on the role, though at a reduced rate of pay. The following April a ruling handed down by an Industrial Court awarded corporation bus conductresses equal pay after six months satisfactory service. The normal working week for women was set at 40 hours compared to 48 hours for their male colleagues. Overtime was to be paid at the male rate. This image shows some of the latest recruits to Liverpool Corporation. (*Mirrorpix*).

Miss Florence Brown (left) and Mrs Ann Dennis, mechanics at London Transport's Chiswick Works, West London. February 1944. (Freddie Cole. *Daily Mirror*).

The scene in Cardiff Labour Exchange as women born in 1920 register for war work. These registrations were not a free for all. It was organised alphabetically according to the first letter of the surname. For example, those with surnames beginning A-C to report between 9.00-10.00am, those D-G between 10.00-11.00am and so on. (*Western Mail Archive*).

The opening of nurseries and nursery schools was a direct response to campaigns organised by mothers who wanted to work but had young children to look after. Local authorities were encouraged provide facilities as well as officially registering 'daily guardians' to look after the children. Daily guardians were placed under Ministry of Health control, their employment considered vital to the war effort.

Every nursery school had a matron who was a State Registered Nurse. The schools were often open 7.00am to 7.00pm on weekdays and 7.00am to around 1.00pm on Saturdays. In the larger schools, the children were divided into nurseries, usually one for those aged six months to two years, and another for the two to five years group. Each child had their own apron, towel, and flannel, as well as a peg to hang their coat on. In many areas of the country, the first job on a Monday morning was to delouse the kids. (*Daily Mirror*).

(Right) One of a new intake of female munitions workers turning a gun barrel. Passed by the censor on 18 June 1941. (*Swansea Evening Post*).

(Above left). Cutting track drive sprockets, possibly for Valentine tanks. October 1942. (*Daily Mirror*).
(Above right). Mrs Slim, aged 72, of Smethwick, was one of many senior citizens working for the war effort. She worked five hours every morning operating drilling or milling machines. Writing in the *Daily Mirror* on Tuesday, 21 April 1942, Bill Greig mentioned an 80-year-old lady who was working in the canteen at a factory in Birmingham. (*Birmingham Evening Despatch*).

Working on a Hawker Typhoon fighter at the Gloster Aircraft Factory, Hucclecote. The Typhoon proved its worth as an interceptor. It was the only aircraft in the RAF capable of catching the Luftwaffe's new Fw 190 at low altitude, and the first two Messerschmitt Me 210 fighter-bombers were also brought down by Typhoons. (*Mirrorpix*).

Assembling cylinder studs on a Merlin engine at the Ford shadow factory at Eccles. Ford were brought into Merlin programme due to the company's experience with mass production. It was also vital that components from similar engines built at Eccles or by Rolls-Royce, Derby, or by Packard in the USA should be fully interchangeable. Eccles produced its first Merlin XX engines in June 1941. (*Daily Herald*).

A worker at the Armstrong Whitworth factory at Whitley, Berkshire, inspecting the coolant and oil radiators of a Merlin XX 1280 HP V12 engine prior to it being fitted to a Lancaster bomber. (*Western Mail*).

(Opposite page bottom). A tank from the 11th Armoured Division pays a visit to the Royal Ordnance Factory at Kirkby, near Liverpool. ROF Kirkby employed up to 20,000 people, many of them women. (*Liverpool Echo*).

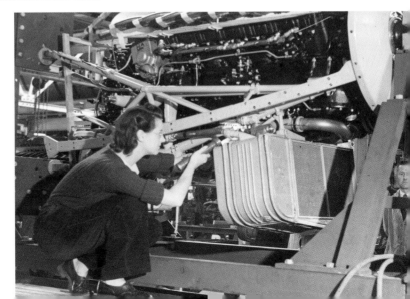

The original entire nine-strong Women Pilots' Section of the Air Transport Auxiliary at the de Haviland factory. Along with leader Miss Pauline Gower are Miss Mona Friedlander, Joan Hughes, Mrs Winifred Crossley, the Honourable Mrs Fairweather, Mrs G Patterson, Marion Wilberforce, Miss Cunnison, and Miss Rosemary Rees.

A total of 165 women pilots served with the ATA. The aircraft they flew from manufacturers to military airfields were unarmed, often lacked some of their instruments and radios. Mary Ellis flew 76 different types of aircraft, often taking off with the manual on her lap. Diana Barnardo Walker delivered 260 Spitfires to RAF bases. Molly Rose flew 486 aircraft and survived a crash involving a Fairey Swordfish torpedo bomber when it experienced a total engine failure.

Fifteen women ATA pilots were killed, the most famous being Amy Johnson (pictured left). On 5 January 1941, whilst delivering an Airspeed Oxford from Prestwick to RAF Headlington in poor weather conditions, Johnson veered off course, ran out of fuel, and bailed out into the Thames Estuary. She was seen alive in the water and in heavy weather and falling snow. Convoy escort HMS Haslemere, attempted to rescue her but to no avail.

By the time the ATA was disbanded in November 1945, its 1153 male and 165 female pilots had delivered more than 309,000 aircraft. (Official. *Westminster Press*).

Initially, the railways trained women to take over unskilled roles, but as the war progressed selected women were trained as passenger guards, signallers, electricians, fitters, boiler cleaners, blacksmiths, and painters, though they were not trained for footplate duties. By the end of the war the London, Midland & Scottish Railway (LMS) alone had 39,000 women on its books, whereas in 1939 the combined total for women employed by the four major railway companies was 25,253.

(Above). Signallers at work at Warmsworth Junction signal box on the former Hull & Barnsley and Great Central Railway Joint in South Yorkshire. The line opened to goods traffic on 1 May 1916, but its four stations, Snaith & Pollington, Sykehouse, Thorpe-in-Balne, and Doncaster York Road, never opened to passenger trains. Warmsworth provided a connection to Yorkshire Main Colliery, which in 1939, set a record producing 1,138,512 tons of coal. (*Daily Mirror*).

(Above). Emily Davies (nearest camera), who was left blind following an air raid, at work inspecting components at an aircraft factory. Visually impaired people were employed by firms such as S U Carburettors, where they could use their sense of touch for certain inspection jobs. (Hackitt, *Birmingham Evening Despatch*).

(Above right). Electrician, Maisy Nicholson works on the wireless aerial of an RAF Marine Branch Air Sea Rescue launch fitting out at the John I Thornycroft, Hampton Launch Works. Thornycroft was situated on Platt's Eyot, an island in the Thames on the reach between Moseley Lock and Sunbury Lock. (Freddie Cole, *Daily Mirror*).

Grace Shultz shows off her skills with an oxy acetylene torch. Great Yeldham, Essex, February 1944. (*Daily Mirror*).

Forging chains for the Royal Navy. March 1941. (*Mirrorpix*).

Mrs Taylor (48) of Bury, Lancashire, gets to grips with firing a Cornish boiler. (Official. *Mirrorpix*).

By 1942 the Forestry Commission was experiencing a labour short even though about 1200 members of the WLA were already working for it. The outcome was the formation of the Women's Timber Corps (WTC) and though the WLA remained responsible for administration and finding suitable recruits, the WTC had a separate identity including wearing a beret.

After an initial training period of four and six weeks, a Lumber Jill, as they were nicknamed, could find herself posted to anywhere in the UK. The work was heavy, the women earning between 35s (£1.75p) and 46s (£2.30p) a week tree felling, and 50s

(£2.50p) a week measuring, a highly skilled job estimating the amount of timber a tree would yield. Jobs undertaken by the WTC included all aspects of forestry work as well as driving tractors, working with teams of horses, surveying, and operating sawmills.

The WTC was divided into nine areas, and during 1943 reached its maximum strength of around 6000 women. It was disbanded in 1946.

WTC members Betty Lewis and Peggy Clarke, both from Gateshead, at work in a Manchester sawmill. Some of these women were skilled enough to be posted to liberated areas of Germany to get sawmills up and running again. (*Mirrorpix*).

The scene in January 1944. A ropewalk crew (possibly Jessie Taylor and Betty Marshall) make ready to close and form a length of rope. Ropewalks could be lengthy places. (Mirrorpix).

A wartime-trained crew of three women working a pair of narrow boats on the Grand Union Canal. The photograph was taken at King's Langley, Hertfordshire. (*Daily Mirror*).

A role that quickly fell to women was sweeping chimneys. Women also took over as coal merchants. (*Mirrorpix*).

Mum's Army

It was not just men who responded to Anthony Eden's broadcast to join the Local Defence Volunteers, better known by many of us as the Home Guard or Dad's Army. Women too were among those who were reporting to local police stations within minutes of Eden's appeal.

However, it had never been the Government's intention that women should enrol. A strange concept given that many women were already working in munitions, or in civil defence, and others were enlisting in the women's armed forces.

In June 1940, the Government went as far as to announce that women could not be enrolled into the ranks of the Home Guard. The same month the Upper Thames Patrol was established, and, as male recruits were thin on the ground, it readily accepted women. Also, many Home Guard units gratefully

accepted offers by local Girl Guides units to run messages for them. The Government even rejected the valid arguments put forward by none other than the C-in-C Home Forces, General Sir Edmund Ironside, as to why, given the then parlous state of what was left of the regular army in Britain, women should not only be allowed to enrol in the Local Defence Volunteers, but also armed.

Even so, many Home Guard units were sympathetic and enrolled women in support roles such as drivers, and messengers. In November 1941, the Government forbade the women from carrying weapons even though many were excellent shots. They were given the unfortunate title of 'nominated women' but were not issued with uniforms, their only evidence of membership being a small broach. There were a few exceptions. The women of the Air Ministry Auxiliary Section

Recruits sign on for Slough Women's Home Defence Unit. (David McLelland Snr, *Daily Mirror*).

for example, were each issued with a navy-blue boiler suit, a navy-blue fore-and-aft forage cap, the two ornamental buttons on the front of which could be unbuttoned when the weather was poor to let down ear flaps. The ensemble was finished off with the wearer sporting a steel helmet and a general service respirator complete with haversack carry bag. By the end of 1942 it is estimated that 50,000 women were unofficially serving with the Home Guard.

Not to be outdone, the independent Women's Home Defence Corps (WHDC) came into being and some Home Guard units were willing to provide them with training. By the beginning of March 1943, it was estimated there were around 30,000 women in more than 200 units. Many had received weapons training, though they were realistic in their aims of being allowed to take over support roles such as drivers, clerks, telephone operators, wireless telegraphists, messengers, cooks, and first aid providers, thereby releasing men for combat duty.

Dr Edith Summerskill, Labour MP for Fulham West, handy with a shotgun, and an active campaigner for equal rights, hounded the Secretary of State for War and the War Office alike, urging official recognition and for all the women to be fully integrated into the Home Guard.

With the Secretary of State for War expected to make a statement in Parliament, Miss G Courtney, secretary of the Mayfair section of the WHDC told the Daily Mirror.

"In the meantime, many of our ranks are getting tired of waiting for official recognition and are joining other women's services. It seems a waste of time for them to change when they are already banded together in organised groups. We have been promised that attention will be drawn to the matter, but it is still under consideration."

In April 1943, the Government finally relented allowing women into the Home Guard though still in support roles though now their official 'uniform' was upgraded to a badge. Some women went ahead and kitted themselves out with an unofficial uniform at their own expense. However, Summerskill and Dame Helen Gwynne-Vaughan continued to campaign for full recognition and the issuing of proper uniforms.

They did however secure a letter of thanks for the women's contribution from King George VI on the standing down of the Home Guard in 1944.

Girl Guides enlisted to deliver messages to members of a Home Guard unit. 22 October 1940. (*Mirrorpix*).

Mrs. W C Thiele (right) and Mrs. P Bartlett of the Upper Thames River Patrol (Home Guard) at Maidenhead. January 1941. (*Mirrorpix*)

A Home Guard sergeant takes rifle drill. Many recruits in rural WHDC units were already excellent markswomen. November 1941. (*Daily Mirror*).

Sergeant E Robinson takes members of the London Savings Bank for target practice. (*Daily Mirror*).

Training in unarmed combat for the London Savings Bank unit. (*Daily Mirror*).

Get Fell In

During the Great War, women were not given the opportunity to join the armed forces until 1917 when the Women's Auxiliary Army Corps (WAAC) and the Women's Royal Naval Service (WRNS) were established. The following year the Women's Royal Air Force (WRAF) was founded.

However, they were soon disbanded. The WRNS went during 1919, the WRAF in 1920 and the last active unit of the WAAC in 1921. Only the self-financing First Aid Nursing Yeomanry carried on throughout the interwar period.

During 1938 the UK Government announced a doubling of the size of the Territorial Army and the re-establishment of a women's service in the guise of the Auxiliary Territorial Service (ATS). Obviously, the women were to be precluded from combat roles, though they could take over as cooks, mess room orderlies, staff car drivers,

and so on. During 1939 both the WRNS and the Women's Auxiliar y Air Force (WAAF) were reformed, though again the roles the women would be allowed to undertake were considered unskilled and non-combatant.

As the war progressed it soon became apparent that women were more than capable of undertaking a vast array of jobs, though only the female members of the Special Operations Executive (SOE) were trained for combat and to kill the enemy.

In December 1941, a second National Service Act was passed. Unmarried women aged 20-30 and childless widows became liable for conscription into the armed forces though there was the option of joining the Women's Land Army. Men up to the age of 60 became liable for some form of National Service including military for those up to the age of 51.

Miss Bridget Jackson, of Clay Cross Hall, Derbyshire, the County Chief Commandant of the Women's Auxiliary Territorial Service (ATS), accompanied by Mrs. J B Marsden-Smedley, the Senior Commandant, inspecting members at a parade in the Drill Hall, Derby, 18 November 1938. (*Derby Telegraph*).

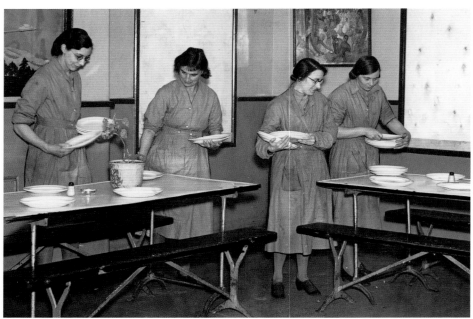

Just eight days after the declaration of war, the *Derb Evening Telegraph* was invited along to Normanton Barracks to see the types of jobs ATS personnel were doing. In those early days, duties included preparing food in the cook house and acting as messroom orderlies. 11 September 1939. (*Derby Telegraph*).

ATS field kitchen set up at Ashbourne Road Methodist Schools, Derby. 2 March 1940. (*Derby Telegraph*).

On 29 January 1941, the ATS invited the Press to a motor transport depot "Somewhere in the North Midlands." Both images are from the event, which included a vehicle recovery demonstration, as well as the drivers parading to draw their billeting allowance, prior to them setting off to deliver new open top lorries to an army unit in Northern Command. With snow and sleet falling, the drivers wrapped up in several layers of clothing. The recovery image was taken by a staff photographer from the *Derby Evening Telegraph*, and that of the trucks lined up carries a *Lincolnshire Echo* copyright notice.

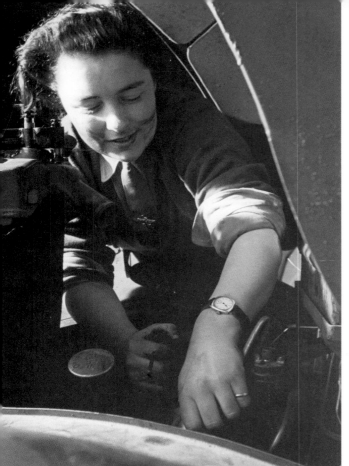

An ATS mechanics at work including at top right, former waitress Edith Care, and pictured below, HRH Princess Elizabeth. (*Mirrorpix*).

Ceaselessly new vehicles roll off the production lines.
Army units await them, the ATS deliver them

(Above) Publicising ATS convoy work. (Official,
Daily Mirror). (Below). The ATS recruiting team pay
a visit to Ranby's Department Store, Victoria Street,
Derby, 23 August 1941. (*Derby Telegraph*).

Page 4 of the *Daily Mirror* edition for Saturday, 14 March 1942, carries a story reporting the arrival at camp of the first intake of 20 to 21-year-old women conscripts for service with the ATS. Personal luggage was limited to a maximum of 15lb (6.8kg). On arrival the women were issued with a khaki greatcoat, overall, stockings, and cap. They were also given shoes, a mug, and a groundsheet.

The first arrival was Betty Harris, a solicitor's secretary from Bournemouth, who made her way by road. The remainder came by train. The ATS driver sent to pick them up was told to start with those wearing high heels, as those wearing flat heels could start walking toward the camp. (*Mirrorpix*).

The latest in ATS hair styles. April 1941. (*Mirrorpix*).

Trainee predictor operators and height/range finder crews serving with the 1st Anti-aircraft Division are shown around a 3inch QF AA gun. The photograph – under the heading *Gunner Girls*, was published on page 5 of the Wednesday, 21 May 1941 edition of the *Daily Mirror*. The woman on the left is sporting the divisional shoulder flash (nicknamed the flaming Heinkel) of a black aircraft, with a dagger in red coming from its tail. Also, the crown on her lower arm shows she is a senior leader, the ATS equivalent to a Company Sergeant Major. The image carries a file date of 23 April 1941, the month the ATS received full military status though its members were paid one-third less than men of the same or equivalent rank. (Official. *Daily Mirror*).

At the end of 1941, the 137th (Mixed) Heavy AA Regiment was formed and later attached to the 33rd (Western) AA Brigade on Merseyside. Here, members of the ATS operate a height/range finder. (Ball, *Liverpool Echo*).

Members of the ATS at the experimental gunnery camp at Manorbier, Wales, training on a kinotheodolite. The device recorded shell bursts from a heavy anti-aircraft gun on film, in relation to the altitude and azimuth of a moving target. Once the film was developed, the accuracy and effectiveness of a gun and its crew could be accessed, and errors corrected. The instructor is subaltern Joan Gotter, at time the only member of the ATS qualified as a gunnery instructor. October 1942. (Official. *Reach plc*).

(Above) ATS members of a mixed HAA battery near Prestwich, shared day picket duty with the men. However, the women did not carry firearms. Night picket duty was the sole preserve of male members of the battery. (Mirrorpix). (Below). ATS members of a mixed heavy anti-aircraft battery based in the North-East, run to their assigned stations during a practice alert for the benefit of the Press. The image is dated 28 November 1941, indicating it was taken at a battery belonging to the 135th (Mixed) Heavy AA Regiment. (*Newcastle Chronicle & Journal*).

Following successful trials, the decision was taken in December 1941 for members of the ATS to be recruited and deployed to searchlight units. In July 1942, the 26th Searchlight Regiment (London Electrical Engineers) became a 'Mixed' regiment. During October 1942, 301 Battery was transferred to the newly raised 93rd (Mixed) Searchlight Regiment, Royal Artillery. They were soon joined by A and B Troops of 339 Battery as the new regiment converted from 'Mixed' to virtually all-female. By the time the transformation was completed, the only males left in the regiment was its Commanding Officer and the senior officers in each of the batteries. (*Mirrorpix*).

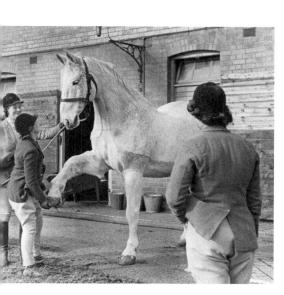

Above). Members of the ATS working at the Army Remount Centre, Melton Mowbray, Leicestershire. (*Mirrorpix*). (Right). Fresh milk courtesy of Mildred the cow. (*Liverpool Echo*).

Window shopping. Members of the ATS looking to the future when the war will be over, and they can amass the coupons to buy civilian underwear. Women were provided with the equivalent of a demob suit, though they were given the option of taking £12 10s (£12.50p) in cash plus 56 clothing coupons. Over the course of the war, the annual clothing coupon allocation shrank, though it was not until the period 1 September 1945 to 30 April 1946, that it reached an all-time low of just 24 coupons per person. Fashion reflected the making of modern women. With rationing still in place, skirts, and hairstyles, went shorter and restrictive corseted styles gave way to more flowing, practical garments. (*Daily Mirror*).

Transit facilities for up to 700 members of the ATS at a time, were opened in Bloomsbury, London, during early 1942. (*Mirrorpix*).

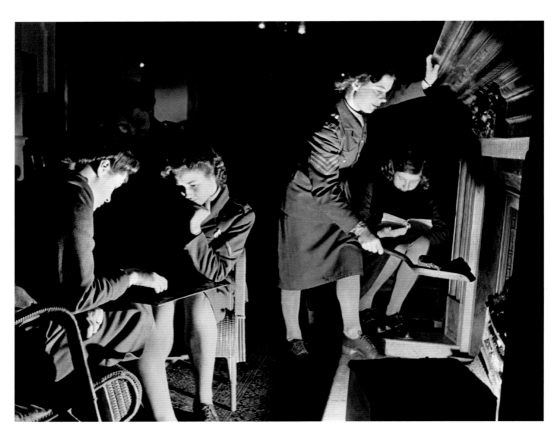

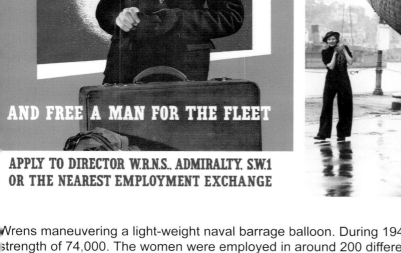

WOMEN'S ROYAL NAVAL SERVICE

JOIN THE **Wrens**

AND FREE A MAN FOR THE FLEET

APPLY TO DIRECTOR W.R.N.S., ADMIRALTY. S.W.1
OR THE NEAREST EMPLOYMENT EXCHANGE

Wrens maneuvering a light-weight naval barrage balloon. During 1944, the WRNS reached its maximum strength of 74,000. The women were employed in around 200 different jobs. One of the more unusual was their involvement in *Operation Outward*, an attack on Germany using balloons that either released incendiary bombs or trailed a wire in the hope it would snag a high voltage power line causing a phase-to-phase outage.

The reason the Royal Navy became involved was because they were sitting on a stockpile of around 100,000 weather balloons. These balloons were ideal for the operation as, unlike barrage balloons, they were easy to move around by hand.

In early March 1942, using the cover story that they were a newly raised boom defence unit, six Royal Navy and Royal Marine officers along with 80 Royal Marines, seven Wren officers and 140 Wren other ranks, were posted to HMS *Beehive*, a shore establishment at Felixstowe.

Launching commenced on 20 March from the Felixstowe Ferry Golf Club and four months later a second launch site was established at Oldstairs Bay. By the time operation ended on 7 February 1944, the unit had launched 96,625 balloons, sometimes up to 1000 a day. A further series of launchings took place between 29 April and 4 September 1944, during which 6517 balloons were released.

The unit's greatest success came on 12 July 1942, when the Bohlen power station was destroyed by fire following the failure of a circuit breaker after an overhead power line had been struck by a wire. (Official. *Reach plc*).

A Wren engineering artificer at work in a machine shop on a naval base. (*Mirrorpix*).

WRNS wireless telegraphists were trained to send and receive Morse code messages at 25 words per minute. Some were involved on Y intercept work on wireless traffic between U boats other German ships, and Wrens with exceptional language skills, and/or the ability to solve puzzles and cryptic crosswords under test conditions, could find themselves posted to HMS *Pembroke*, one of the numerous cover names for the Government Code and Cypher School (GC&CS) at Bletchley Park.

There, they joined women from the ATS, WAAFS and civilian life working on the breaking of Axis ciphers, notably the German Enigma and Lorenz codes. (Official. *Mirrorpix*).

Wrens tackle a heavy repair to an anti-submarine net. Splicing wire was not an easy task, even for a man. The photograph is believed to have been taken on the Clyde. (*Daily Mirror*).

From 1941 onwards, Wren ratings took over responsibility for operating many of the small craft that the Royal Navy employed around its bases. They were also issued with bell-bottomed trousers to replace their skirts. (Above). Wren Yvonne "Inches" Trewin, leaps ashore to make fast as the duty boat she was working on comes alongside at Devonport. November 1944. (Official. *Daily Mirror*).

WAAF plotters at work in the operations room at RAF Fighter Command HQ, Bentley Priory, Middlesex. The movements of friendly and enemy aircraft alike were plotted on the large table map using information supplied by the Home Chain Radar stations and Royal Observer Corps. (Official. *Daily Mirror*).

Flight mechanics keep the tail of a Hurricane fighter firmly on the ground.
June 1943. (*Mirrorpix*).

Parachutes are inspected prior to folding, packing, and being issued to air crew. (Official. *Mirrorpix*).

WAAF and RAF ground crew enjoy a bit of down time. June 1942. (*Mirrorpix*).

In January 1941, Balloon Command were asked to consider a suggestion that the flying of balloons could be undertaken by WAAFs. It was demanding work, the balloons had to be manned twenty-four hours a day and were often flown in the most appalling weather conditions.

There had been some technical improvements to equipment, including the mechanization of some aspects of handling but Balloon Command still thought the job required physical strength not usually possessed by women. However, it was decided to have a trial run.

Thus, on a cold, wet, morning in April 1941, twenty WAAF volunteers attended their first course at Cardington. By the end of June, they had proved their worth and the Sheffield barrage was chosen as the site for a full-scale experiment. In July, the women took over D Flight of 939 Squadron and by the end of the year all balloons, except for those on isolated sites had been handed over to the WAAF.

Thousands of WAAF officers, NCOs and air women were transferred to Balloon Command, releasing their male colleagues for front line service. Balloon Command went on a recruit drive. It was open to healthy women of a minimum height of 5ft 1in (1.55metres) and up to 43 years-of-age. The minimum pay was three shillings (15p) a day, all found. Any married woman who enlisted and whose husband was in the services continued to receive her allowances and was to be granted leave to coincide with that of her husband, subject to service conditions.

At first, the substitution of WAAFs for airmen on balloon sites was not as straightforward as it might appear. Even though technical improvements in balloon handling meant that physical strength was no longer a prime consideration, it still took sixteen WAAFs to replace ten men. Also, RAF balloon crews were integrated into military defence schemes whereas the WAAFs were non-combatants. (*Manchester Evening News*).

WOMEN WANTED
to take over the
BALLOON BARRAGE

The nightmare of Nazi airmen is Britain's balloon barrage. That's why it is one of the most important jobs in the country to keep those silver fish flying! And the WAAF have proved they can take over this important front-line job from the RAF!

It's a fine, healthy life for women who are fit and strong and fond of the open air. You must be 5' 1" or over, and aged between 17½ and 43. After a short training course, you will be posted to a balloon site. Sites are usually in or near a town. There you will live and work in a small community of about a dozen or so. When fully trained your minimum pay is 3/- a day *and all found.*

In addition to balloon operation, there are many other interesting trades open now in the WAAF. Every woman not doing vital work is asked to volunteer.

A Serviceman's wife does NOT lose her allowance on joining up, and she IS granted her leave to coincide with her husband's leave, subject only to urgent Service considerations.

Go to a Recruiting Centre* or Employment Exchange for fuller information. If you are in work, *they* will find out whether you can be spared from it. If you cannot go at once, send in the coupon.

When this girl joined the WAAF six months ago, to become a balloon operator, she was badly under weight. Now she's back to normal. "You can tell them from me, it's a grand life!" she says.

*Single girls born between January 1st, 1918, and June 30th, 1922, come under the National Service Act and *must* go to the Employment Exchange, *not* a Recruiting Centre.

WAAF

297 Oxford Street, London, W.1	3010 *AR 10*

Please send me full information about the trade of Balloon Operator in the WAAF.

Mrs.⎫
Miss⎬ _____
                           Cross out "Mrs." or "Miss"

Address _____

County_____ Date of birth_____
                                      In confidence

(Above left). A WAAF operated balloon site at the Tower of London. (*Mirrorpix*). (Below). Repairing a balloon belonging to the Derby barrage. 1941. (*Derby Telegraph*).

WAAF Iris Miriam Deeley spent much of Sunday, 13 February 1944, with her fiancée William Quill, and missed the last train from Charring Cross to RAF Kidbrooke. After contacting her unit, she caught a train to Lewisham. Witnesses reported seeing her with a soldier.

The following day her body was discovered on an allotment near to West Hall station, Eltham. She had been raped and strangled. All the police had to go on were footprints from an exceptionally large pair of boots. Six days later, a keen-eyed police constable spotted a young soldier wearing medal ribbons from campaigns fought long before the soldier had been born. Gunner Ernest James Harman Kemp RA was arrested.

Kemp was AWOL from his unit and some of Iris's possessions were found in his kitbag. The footprints also matched. Kemp was executed at Wandsworth Prison on 6 June. (*Daily Mirror*).

Some of the 600 Polish WAAFs stationed in the UK. Many had harrowing stories to tell of their escapes from the Nazis. Others were held in the Soviet Union and released, coming to the UK via Persia and Africa, when the agreement was reached to form the Polish Forces in the West. One Polish airman who had paid an off-chance visit to a seaside resort ran into his wife and daughter who were both serving in the WAAFs. He had not seen them since his escape from Poland in September 1939. (Illustrations Bureau, *Liverpool Echo*).

Former member of the First Aid Nursing Yeomanry (FANY) Odette Sansom at her wedding to Captain Peter Churchill. However, Sansom's membership of that organisation was a cover for her role as an agent in the Special Operations Executive (SOE).

Born in Amiens, France, in 1912, in the Spring of 1942, Sansom answered an Admiralty appeal for postcards and photographs of the region around Boulogne. However, by mistake Sansom sent he photographs direct to the War Office where they landed on the desk of Colonel Maurice Buckmaster of the SOE, who in due course persuaded her to join.

SOE operatives were trained sabotage, intelligence gathering, communications, hand-to-hand combat, to be resourceful, and think clearly in stressful situations. They were planted in occupied countries in Europe and Asia under assumed identities. They were the only women of His Majesty's forces permitted a combat role.

Under the code name Lise, she landed in France on 2 November 1942, and contacted Peter Churchill, head of SOE in the area around Cannes. All went until 16 April 1943, when the pair were arrested. Though interrogated and tortured on numerous occasions by the Gestapo, she refused to betray other SOE operatives. Odette and Churchill stuck to their story that they were a husband-and-wife team and that he was the nephew of the Prime Minister.

Odette eventually finished up in Ravensbruck Concentration Camp where she was held in the punishment block on starvation rations. As the Allies neared the camp, its commandant Fritz Suhren took Odette and surrendered to US forces, thinking the Churchill connection might save him from being tried for war crimes. It did not, Suhren was executed in 1950.

Odette Sansom was the first woman to be awarded the George Cross. She was also made a Chevalier de la Legion d'honneur by France. In 1950 her exploits hit the silver screen in the movie *Odette* starring Anna Neagle and Trevor Howard.

Our image shows Odette and Peter Churchill on their wedding day. (McNeill, *Daily Mirror*).

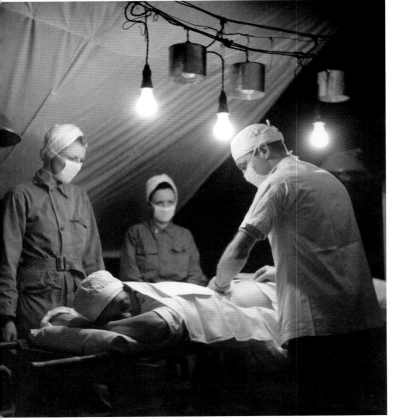

The first three African American female nurses of the American Red Cross to arrive in the UK. Segregation in the United States was such that even in late 1941, the American Red Cross was informed by the surgeons general of Army and Navy, that the only blood acceptable to the services was that taken from white donors.

In January 1942, the US War Department agreed to accept blood from coloured donors though it insisted on the adherence to segregation. White blood for the white folks, coloured blood for the coloured folks. Despite there being no racial difference in blood. Despite the pioneering work done by Dr Charles Drew, Medical Director of the American Red Cross blood bank programme on methods for storing and preserving blood for later use in transfusions. Dr Drew was an African American. (*Mirrorpix*).

US Army field hospital in Wales. The facility included operating theatres, x-ray unit and dental department. February 1944. (*Mirrorpix*).

The Blitz

The Blitz is usually defined as the period of the heavy bombing of British cities from 7 September 1940 until mid- May 1941 when Luftwaffe units were withdrawn to prepare for the invasion of Russia. The Blitz was a final attempt to finish Britain off following Germany's failure to win either of their Kanalkampf (Channel War) and Battle of Britain campaigns. It too would be a strategic failure.

During the period we now call the Phoney War, the Luftwaffe carried out many 'tip and run' raids, often by single aircraft testing our defences or unloading unused bombs from combat patrols. However, the first bomb to be dropped on Britain was at just before 8.00am on 24 September 1939, when a house at Headlington, near Oxford, suffered a direct hit from a practice bomb accidently released by a RAF aircraft. The bomb failed to detonate but even so, a young evacuee was seriously injured.

Saturday 7 September 1940, and the weather was clear. At 4.00pm the coast long chain radar detected a large enemy force heading toward the UK. The RAF was no longer the primary target, and Observer Corps posts were soon verifying a new objective – London. Every available fighter 11 Group could muster was scrambled and they needed to be as the bombers had friends with them in the shape of 600 fighters.

The concentration point for the 318 bombers was London's docklands. By the time the raiders left, warehouses had been transformed into infernos and the residential areas of Wapping, Bow, Silver Town, West Ham and Bermondsey had suffered heavy damage. At 8.00pm the raiders returned, and by the time the all-clear sounded at 5.00am, nine miles of waterfront was ablaze, and 448 people had been killed. London would be bombed for the next 56 consecutive nights. The Blitz had begun.

Mid-November saw the implementation of the Luftwaffe's change in tactics by extending the Night Blitz to the provinces. On the night of the 14th, Coventry was raided by 552 aircraft in an attack that lasted eleven hours. Fires quickly took hold, and as they flew over the Channel, crews of some of the later aircraft mistook   a faint red glow in the sky for what they thought might be some sort of night fighter beacon. It was Coventry burning. On the ground, the glow could be seen from as far away as Birmingham, Rugby, and Derby.

In Coventry, chaos reigned. The Civil Defence Control Centre had taken a direct hit and local communications now relied almost entirely upon the undoubted bravery of teenagers and boy scouts who made their way through mayhem relaying messages to police, fire crews, first aid parties and rescue squads.

Adding to Coventry's problems was the fact that all roads in and out were blocked with debris and the railway line severely damaged. Though help

Spotters get acquainted with aircraft recognition. September 1940. (*Daily Mirror*).

was on its way from surrounding towns, as well as a convoy from the London Fire Brigade, it would be hours before any would get through. When the relief columns eventually arrived, some discovered that they could not connect to Coventry's water supply due to their vehicles having different diameter fittings. At the time, there was no standard for fire hydrants etc, local authorities did their own thing. The result was equipping of every fire appliance as soon as practical with at least six different connectors.

So devastating was the raid that the government lifted reporting restrictions and allowed the target to be named. The image of a city where one third of its centre, including its cathedral, had been destroyed completely went round the world and aroused strong feelings and Nazi Germany scored

Gillian Turner was awarded the George Medal for gallant conduct, when during the raid of 20 September 1940 on London, she drove an AFS lorry for three hours from fire to fire. It was loaded with petrol for refuelling trailer pumps. (George Greenwell. *Daily Mirror*).

an own goal. A new word entered the lexicon of warfare – Coventration – the destruction of a city by aerial bombardment. What was not reported was that the local authority lost control of the situation and troops called in to clear the rubble were also there to maintain order.

Another lesson learned from Coventry was the need for crash evacuations. A system whereby those made homeless in a blitz-type raid could be evacuated quickly and effectively instead of being left to their own devices. One of the first cities to establish a crash evacuation plan was Hull, though by January 1941, the city was preparing a more detailed scheme organised by their Director of Education, R C Moore.

Before the end of November 1940, many cities including, Bristol, Liverpool, Southampton, and Birmingham had been subjected to heavy raids. During December, weather conditions were such that the Luftwaffe were grounded for much of the time. However, they still mounted eleven major and five moderately heavy raids including what later became known in Manchester as the Christmas Blitz. During this period, London suffered three major and twelve light raids.

Before the year was out, the Press and Censorship Bureau introduced a new procedure, blocking the release of images featuring damage to well-known locations. The '28-day & 2nd raid rule,' was intended to deny the Luftwaffe Intelligence Section information useful in compiling reports on the effectiveness of specific raids. It also plays merry havoc with modern researchers as the dates often found on the reverse of 'sensitive' photographs have little to do with when they were taken, and more to do with when they were cleared for publication, lodged in a newspaper's library, or when they were eventually published. In some instances, the Censorship Bureau held on to photographs for several months.

On the night of Saturday 11 January 1941, London was once again the target. Bank station took a direct hit, the bomb detonating in the booking hall. The blast wave was funnelled down the escalator causing the roof to collapse and blowing passengers into the path of an oncoming train. Though the train's automatic brake engaged it was too late for some of the people in its path. A rescue party from Liverpool Street station arrived and within three hours the dead and injured had been taken away. To get road traffic moving, a temporary bridge was thrown across what soon became known as 'the largest crater in London.' The bridge was officially opened by the Lord Mayor on 3 February. By May the roadway had been repaired and the bridge removed.

During 1942-43, there were less than thirty raids on London, though 1944 opened with the Little Blitz. The Luftwaffe had managed to assemble a hotchpotch of 550 aircraft in northern France but as many of the crews were untrained a pathfinder unit had to be employed. On 21 January, a two-wave attack totalling 447 aircraft failed mainly due to poor navigation and only 32 tonnes of bombs fell on the capital. By May 1944, the Luftwaffe in France had just 144 operational aircraft available for raids.

At 3.50am on 13 June 1944, the sirens warned of an impending attack on London. Anti-aircraft batteries opened fire on a single aircraft that crashed a few minutes later, on open land at Barking. About thirty minutes after that a second plane crashed but this time it came down in a populated area causing casualties. It was two or three days before the authorities realised that the Luftwaffe had deployed a new weapon the V1, a rocket powered, pilotless flying bomb armed with a 1000kg warhead. The weapon was equipped with an autopilot, and when the fuel ran out, the distinctive sound made by its engine stopped, and it plummeted to earth and exploded. The Germans calculated how much fuel a V1 would need to reach its intended target area, aim it in the general direction and launch. By the end of June 660 V1s had hit London, others had come down in the Portsmouth/Southampton area.

The Germans instructed their agents including Eddie Chapman, to monitor where the V1s landed and report the location and damage caused. Only thing was that Eddie, and the other agents were all working for the British. With careful coordination, the agents' reports for damage caused by V1s landing around northwest London, were matched to the times of V1s landing in southeast London. The idea was to convince the Germans they were overshooting. They would then adjust fuel levels and the V1s would fall short of much of the capital. To lend credibility to Chapman's reports, he was allowed to send photographs of real damage caused by V1s to Germany via Lisbon. Chapman was the only Englishman ever to be awarded an Iron Cross by Adolf Hitler.

As the frequency of this type of attack increased it was decided to move the anti-aircraft batteries to the coast where, by sheer weight of firepower, they destroyed more than half of all incoming V1s. Fighter aircraft also intercepted incoming V1s, pilots closing then using a wing to flip the weapons off course.

Winston Churchill and his wife Clementine travel back along the Thames by boat after visiting the devastated Docklands area. September 1940. (*Mirrorpix*).

By the end of August, the British Second Army had overrun the V1 launch sites in the Pas-de-Calais, forcing the Germans to adopt the practice of air-launching the weapons from Heinkel III bombers. More than 700 were launched by this method, though many exploded upon release taking their mothership with them. Others were launched at targets further afield including Manchester and Oldham, where 27 people died in one explosion.

On 8 September, mysterious explosions destroyed parts of Chiswick and Epping. The was no siren, no warning, just huge explosions followed by the noise of the rocket engines then sonic booms from the upper atmosphere. The first V2s had landed. The V2 was a 14 tonne, 45 foot (13.7 metre) long rocket launched from a mobile platform. It travelled at supersonic speed which meant it landed and exploded before anyone heard it arrive. It flew too high and too fast for any RAF fighter to intercept it or anti-aircraft battery to shoot it down. In all, 518 V2s landed upon London, killing 2274 people, and seriously injuring 6000 others. The last V2 landed on 25 March 1945 at Orpington. A few hours later, the last V1 came down. It fell on Chislehurst.

The last raid occurred on the night of 17/18 March 1945, when the Luftwaffe sortied eighteen aircraft. Eleven of them crossed the east coast between Scarborough and Walton-on-the-Naze to attack Hull, resulting in twelve people killed and 22 seriously injured. The total civilian casualties from raids and V weapon attacks were 60,595 killed and 86,182 seriously injured.

A London Fire Brigade Mobile District Control in action. October 1940. (*Mirrorpix*).

The morning of 15 November 1940. People make their way through the still smouldering ruins of Coventry. In the foreground lies the remains of an AFS trailer pump. Beyond that are the twisted remnants of a corporation bus. On the right stands the burnt-out shell of the Owen Owen department store, its conflagration, after that of the cathedral, considered by locals the second most 'famous' fire of the raid. (*Birmingham Post & Mail*).

In the aftermath of the raid on Coventry, a Salvation Army mobile canteen is on hand providing tea and sandwiches to those in need. (*Coventry Telegraph*).

LAST EDITION

Our Office in Hertford Street is Open Daily for Business as Usual

The Midland Daily Telegraph

Newsagents are requested to hand in their orders at Hertford Street as usual

No. 15,429.　　　TUESDAY, 19 NOVEMBER, 1940.　　　ONE PENNY.

ALL AID RUSHED TO COVENTRY
"But people must help themselves"

EMERGENCY COMMITTEE DISCUSS MEASURES FOR STRAIGHTENING OUT THE WRECKAGE

BOMB-WRECKED Coventry, you must give yourselves first aid until the authorities, who are urging every muscle to help, can bring the full force of assistance to you.

Government technicians and high military officials, together with all the chiefs of Corporation departments, were present at yesterday's meeting of Coventry National Emergency Committee, when further measures for straightening out the wreckage in the city were discussed at length.

While no effort in the capacity of the country to provide is to be spared to help Coventry, Alderman G. E. Hodgkinson, vice-chairman of the Emergency Committee, told the "Midland Daily Telegraph" after the meeting that for the moment Coventry people must do what they can to help themselves.

"It would be impossible for all the jobs to be tackled at once, and in the meantime people can do — and are doing — a great deal to make their damaged houses habitable," he said.

Restoration of damaged utility services was one of the main points of the discussion and this work, together with repairs to house property, will be the first essential.

Every effort is being made to get slaters and tilers from other parts of the country to come to Coventry's help. The country is being raked to obtain assistance.

FILLING IN THE CRATERS

The labour problem involved in the filling in of bomb craters in roads, and the clearing of debris was considered further in conjunction with the military authorities.

Consideration was also given to improving methods of getting all the essential services into operation.

The question of accommodating industrial workers was debated, and "The Midland Daily Telegraph" was informed that compulsory billeting powers are now being operated.

CLASH ON INDO-CHINA FRONTIER

TOKIO, Tuesday.

"Fighting on a considerable scale" has broken out between French Indo-China and Thailand forces on the frontier, according to a Hanoi report to the Domei (Japanese) news agency to-day.

Thai aircraft are stated to have flown over Indo-Chinese territory. The fighting, adds the report, centres round Pakse, in the Laos Province, but skirmishes are also going on near Vientiann and Savannaket. — Reuter.

London Salutes Coventry

MR. EMIL DAVIES, chairman of the L.C.C., has telegraphed the Mayor of Coventry that the people of London "salute people of Coventry for their proud spirit and high courage, and invite the Mayor to let London know if we can be of assistance."

NEWS IN BRIEF

Will the First Lord of the Admiralty publish in the near future photographs showing the damage done to the Italian Fleet at Taranto? Notice of this question in the House of Commons has been given by Capt. Plugge (Con., Rochester, Chatham).

A charge against John William Cunningham (25), of Broadstone Road, Reddish, of failing to submit himself for a medical examination at Manchester under the provisions of the National Service (Armed Forces) Act was withdrawn at Stockport yesterday.

The death of Professor Ernest William MacBride, Emeritus Professor of London University, who in 1935 at a British Association meeting attacked the Darwinian theory, is announced to-day at the age of 74 at Alton, Hants.

All the violence of the Nazi terror raid failed to destroy completely the matchless beauty of Coventry's Cathedral. The pinnacles and the arched windows stood above the wreckage in poignant, yet elegant grandeur.

PREPARING FOUNDATIONS FOR CITY'S NEW CENTRE

THE Coventry landscape is changing hour by hour as the authorities get more fully into their stride on the work of demolition and the rendering safe of buildings left hanging crazily as the result of last week's air raid devastation.

People who have been privileged to witness the operation have seen history made under their eyes. They have seen the first great strides towards the making of the new Coventry that one day will rise from the present ruins.

So fast have the workmen got on with the job that when those with business in the city centre arrived this morning they found missing whole buildings that were still standing last night.

Huge pieces of machinery were brought into operation to pull down unsafe buildings, and soldiers drafted into the city to help in the great task of clearing up worked side by side with the demolition contractor, for whom no job was too immense.

Among military units taking part to-day were several parties drawn from the Royal Warwickshire Regiment.

The work was still going on this morning among the piles of debris, still smouldering five days after the raid that has shocked the whole world.

EVACUATING THE CHILDREN

Despite the terrifying experiences which were suffered by the population on Thursday, Coventry Education Committee find that the response to their rapidly - organised scheme of evacuation of school children is not meeting with the response expected.

"The Midland Daily Telegraph" was informed this morning that the number of registrations so far received was re-

markably small in the circumstances, and it was obvious that the parents of children were in many instances adhering to their original decision not to be separated from their children.

In view of all the devastation in the city and the large number of schools damaged by Thursday's widespread bombing, this lack of co-operation on the part of parents is, in the circumstances, to be deplored.

NORTH COUNTRY DESTINATION

To-day, however, a large number of children left the city by motor-coach from various points.

They included children from Wheatley-street Infants', the Junior and Commercial Schools of the Technical College, and children of All Saints', Cheylesmore Girls, Christ the King, Canley, Whoberley Juniors and Boys' School, and the majority of these will be billeted in a North Country town.

INSTRUCTIONS TO PARENTS

Parents are asked particularly to notice the following instructions which apply to to-morrow's evacuation scheme:—

Arrangements are being made for a trainload of children to leave the city chiefly from the Foleshill area, the children to be entrained at Foleshill Station at 1.45 p.m., and at Longford Station at 1.50 p.m.

Children must assemble at their schools at the latest by 12 noon, and the following schools are included in Wednesday's arrangements:—

Barkers' Butts; Coundon; Edgwick; Hen Lane; Holbrook Lane; Little Heath; Paradise; Radford; Windmill Road; Foleshill C.E.; Longford; Hill Farm; and the two girls' secondary schools.

Parents are urged to provide a change of underclothing for the children and to ensure that they carry with them their identity and ration cards and gas masks.

Children should, of course, take warm clothing with them, and, if possible, a strong pair of bots, while a pair of Wellingtons should also be included if possessed.

Will parents note particularly that only those children who register at their schools will be permitted to join the party.

Sir Samuel Hoare Returning to Spain

LISBON, Tuesday.

Sir Samuel Hoare, British Ambassador to Spain, has left here by car for Madrid after a visit lasting about a week.

While in Lisbon Sir Samuel conferred with Lord Lothian, British Ambassador to the United States, who is on his way back to Washington, and Sir Walford Selby, British Ambassador to Portugal.—Reuter.

Coloured French subjects are recommended by Lyons radio not to return to German-occupied France

A postman sorts through the mail. Much of it will be returning with him to the sorting office. Smithford Street looking towards Fleet Street, Coventry. (*Coventry Telegraph*).

When much of their home on Highgate Road, Balsall Heath, Birmingham, collapsed during a raid, these people's lives were saved by the fact they had scrambled into a Morrison shelter. (*Birmingham Post & Mail*).

Prams left outside a London tube station as mothers and children seek shelter during a raid. (Palmer, *Daily Mirror*).

Having been bombed out of their home in the East End, Mr and Mrs Katar Singh and their family spent Christmas 1940 in the crypt of Christ Church, Spitalfields. (*Daily Mirror*).

On Christmas Eve 1940, nurses at Westminster Hospital tour the wards singing carols. For hospital staff and patients alike, it would be a night free from bombing due to an unofficial truce arranged in Washington. The German Embassy offered to suspend all raids for the Christmas period provided the British reciprocated. The bombing resumed at 6.45 pm on Boxing Day when 108 aircraft attacked London, though this appears to have been in retaliation for raids carried out earlier in the day by the RAF against Luftwaffe bases. (George Greenwell, *Daily Mirror*).

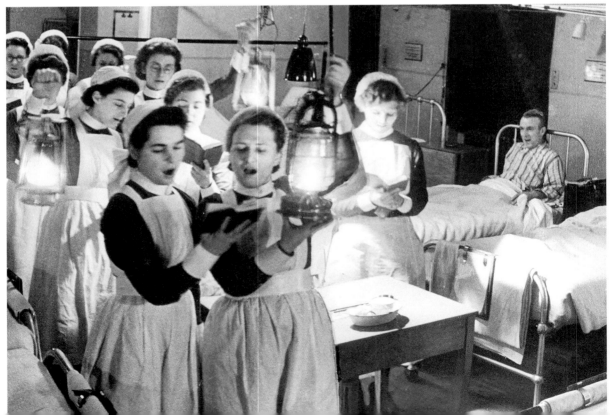

The Second Fire of London

At 6.17 pm, on Sunday 29 December 1940, the lead aircraft of KGr100 (the Luftwaffe equivalent of an RAF pathfinder squadron) dropped its payload of marker incendiaries over the concentration point – the square mile of the city of London. Whenever weather conditions allowed it, KGr100's incendiary fires enabled the aircraft belonging to other units to bomb visually and this would be one of those nights. What would soon be dubbed "The Second Fire of London" or the "HE Fire Blitz" had begun.

Due to an expected weather front that would hinder landing operations at their bases in France, the raid was compressed and lasted just 2hrs 13min. During this time frame 156 bombers dropped 127 tonnes of high explosives (HE) and 22,068 incendiaries, 10,470 of which were delivered by KGr100. By Luftwaffe standards it was not a heavy attack. Synchronicity worked in the Luftwaffe's favour. There was a 50mph westerly wind blowing. Firefighters were hampered by many buildings being locked and barred. There was a lack of firewatchers to deal with incendiaries. The emergency mains water pipe from the Thames was put out of action by a bomb. The Thames was at low ebb and many riverside fires had to be abandoned as fireboats had difficulty reaching them.

At the outbreak of the Second World War, Harry Guy Bartholomew, Editorial Director, and part owner of the *Daily Mirror* was too old for military service. However, in 1940 he volunteered to work on a temporary basis for the Auxiliary Fire Service (AFS). A brilliant picture editor, artist and cartoonist in his own right, Bartholomew recognised publishing potential when he saw it and whenever he went out on fire patrol, he ensured that *Daily Mirror* photographer and fellow AFS firefighter and *Mirror* cameraman George Greenwell went along with him.

At some time during the raid, George, possibly along with Harry Bartholomew, had clambered up more than 500 steps to the top of the dome of St Paul's Cathedral from where he took some of the greatest images of the blitz on London. The cathedral's firewatchers successfully dealt with 27 of the 28 incendiaries that landed. The odd one out crashed through the outer shell of the dome and became lodged dangerously close to some old wooden beams. However, as firewatchers raced to deal with it, the incendiary fell onto the Stone Gallery some 376 steps up from the cathedral floor where it was safely extinguished.

During the night, George photographed the unfolding dramas around St Paul's such as the fires raging along Ave-Maria Lane, Paternoster Row, St Brides Church in Fleet Street, the church of St Lawrence Jewry and the Guildhall. In the early hours on Victoria Embankment, he photographed the remains of a tram that had been ripped apart by the blast wave from a HE bomb. At daybreak he was on hand, taking a series of images recording the recovery of an AFS heavy unit buried beneath tons of debris in City Road.

In all 163 people were killed including sixteen firefighters, and 509 people seriously injured.

During December 1940, the Press and Censorship Bureau introduced a new procedure, blocking the release of images featuring damage to well-known locations. The '28-day & 2nd Raid rule,' was intended to deny the Luftwaffe Intelligence Section information useful in compiling reports on the effectiveness of specific raids.

George's image of what appear to be falling flares. These were designed to ignite five seconds after being dropped. Despite their small size, they produced intense heat and light. (George Greenwell, *Daily Mirror*)

(Opposite page top). From the dome of St Paul's. The view is to the north west. Paternoster Row is in the foreground. (George Greenwell, *Daily Mirror*).

(Opposite page bottom). The west front of St Paul's from the dome. (George Greenwell, *Daily Mirror*).

Though about six hours had passed since the last of the German bombers had turned for home, fires were still raging. This is the scene in Paternoster Row in the early hours of 30 December 1940. (George Greenwell, *Daily Mirror*).

The night of 3 January 1941 was the coldest so far that winter. So cold in fact that during a raid on Bristol, the spray from fire hoses froze. *Bristol Post* chief photographer Jim Facey came across this ladder escape. (Jim Facey, *Bristol Post*).

(Opposite page top). A Ministry of Information van parks up alongside still smouldering ruins following a raid on Bristol. The job of the van's staff was to pass on information regarding any emergency evacuations, advise householders how to contact the local authority regarding repairs to houses, and how to obtain replacement ration books and clothing. (*Bristol Post*).

(Opposite page bottom). The morning after a raid. The staff in the control room at the London Fire Service HQ are listing available appliances and pumps each station can deploy should the raiders return. (*Daily Mirror*).

A scene that played out on thousands of occasions. Householders, salvage whatever they can from their shattered homes. (Jim Facey, *Bristol Post*).

Taking shelter from the bombs in a London
Underground station. A mother tends to her
young son while her daughter settles down
for the night in a bed made from a wooden
fruit crate. (*Mirrorpix*).

Miss Potter holds a maths class at the
Elephant & Castle tube station. (*Mirrorpix*).

Following a heavy raid on their town
during which 1200 houses were
destroyed or rendered uninhabitable,
around three hundred families took up
residence in the Ramsgate tunnels. T
tunnels soon boasted facilities includi
a hospital, greengrocers, a barber's
shop, and a canteen.

The original tunnel had been for railw
use but during the late 1930s, the ma
of Ramsgate applied to the Home Off
for funds to excavate additional tunne
for use as air raid shelters. The first n
ARP tunnel was ready by June 1939.
It was officially opened by the Duke o
Kent. (*Mirrorpix*).

Against Government advice, King George VI and Queen Elizabeth refused to be evacuated. They could regularly be seen visiting those whose homes had been destroyed or rendered uninhabitable by bombing. (Above) Queen Elizabeth chats to the Lord Mayor of Hull, Sydney Herbert Smith, and the Sheriff, Mr Robert Greenwood Tarran, during a visit to the blitzed areas of the city. (*Hull Daily Mail*). (Below) King George VI meets with residents of a bombed area of Birmingham. (*Birmingham Post & Mail*).

Mr C E Mill and his family trundle their way through the devastated streets of Plymouth. The city had suffered heavy raids during the nights of 20th and 21st March 1941. At the City General Hospital, Dr Alison McNairn regained consciousness to find herself up to her neck in debris. Eventually freeing herself, Dr McNairn then worked a 22-hour shift treating injured children, though she herself was suffering excruciating pain from several fractured ribs. She was later awarded the George Medal. (*Daily Mirror*).

At the height of the London Blitz of 16 April 1941, a female member of the AFS makes sure the firefighters around Bolsover Street/Ebury Street, get a much-needed drink of water and when practical a refreshing cuppa. The figure on the left appears to be filming the scene. The red markings indicate the alterations required by the censor before publication is allowed. (George Greenwell, *Daily Mirror*).

The gaping hole torn in the nurses' home at Salford Royal Infirmary during the raid of 1-2 June 1941. Fourteen nurses were killed. Nearby is St Phillip's Church, from where the Reverend James Hussey was walking to comfort the wounded at the hospital, when he too was killed by a bomb. (*Daily Mirror*).

Water main destroyed, the residents in the Shaftsbury Crescent area of Derby eagerly await the arrival of a corporation water cart. August 1941. (*Derby Telegraph*).

Middlesbrough, Bank Holiday Monday, 3 August 1942. At 1.13pm, and almost as soon as the town's air raid sirens had wailed their ominous warning, a Dornier 217 bomber dropped four HE bombs, two of which hit the railway station. One landed immediately in front of locomotive on the 1.20pm train for Newcastle, killing its guard who was crossing the track. The locomotive's fireman was also killed.

There were lucky escapes. As the bombs hit, the seventeen-year-old assistant from the station bookstall was making her way along the subway under the platforms, when a young man pushed her up against the wall protecting her from flying debris. The eighteen-year-old clerk from the booking office on the Redcar platform was stopped by workmen from going onto the platform. Had she not been stopped she would have been on the steps going down to the subway when its tiled wall collapsed.

Evening Gazette chief photographer Teddy Baxter had just gone into the paper's canteen. On hearing the sirens, he dashed up onto the roof just in time to see the plane loose its payload. He rushed downstairs, jumped into a delivery van, and headed for the station.

Teddy took ten images, headed back to the office, developed, and printed them, then put them on a train from Darlington to London and the censors. Teddy then found himself in hot water. The Circulation Manager who was also in charge of the paper's transport, read the riot act. Teddy had brought the van back with three punctured tyres and replacement tyres were hard to come by.

The censors stuck to the two raids, 28 days rule, so it was five and a half weeks before the images were released for publication. They went round the world. Enlargements, 20ft by 15ft (6.1 x 4.57metres), were sent to Australia and New Zealand to boost an appeal for clothing and blankets for bombed-out families. (Teddy Baxter, *Evening Gazette*).

Daily Mirror photographer George Greenwell captures the moment shortly after lunchtime on 30 June 1944, when a V1 detonated in the Aldwych, London. The incident was one of the deadliest, leaving 48 dead and 200 injured.

At the time, Bush House in the Aldwych, was home to the BBC's Empire and European radio services, employing at least 1400 people. Interestingly, the show *Shipmates Ahoy* was going out live and listeners heard the V1 denotate as it landed.

It was here in January 1941, that Victor de Laveleye, director of the Belgian service suggested opening broadcasts to Belgium with the Morse code dot, dot, dot, dash sound for the letter V – in this case meaning V for Victory. By happy coincidence, the opening of Beethoven's *Fifth Symphony* sounds similar. It was soon taken up by all the language services.

Winston Churchill took up his trademark V for Victory sign in public for the first time, during speech on 19 July 1941. Initially, Churchill appears to have been unaware that giving the V sign with the back of his hand facing the observer was an insult. The meaning was eventually pointed out to the great man whereupon he is said to have cried with laughter. Interestingly, the Germans also adopted the V for victory sign.

Powered by an Argus As 109-014 Pulsejet, the *Vergeltungswaffe -1* (Vengeance Weapon 1) went into operational service on 12 June 1944, though all nine that were launched failed to reach England. However, it was a different story the following day when ten flying bombs were launched against London. Of these four crashed on take-off, and two crashed into the Channel. Of the others, the first V1 to land in England hit the village of Swanscombe in Kent. Others came down on Bethnal Green, Sevenoaks and Cuckfield.

The V1 and subsequent V2 campaigns sparked off fresh rounds of evacuations including from Southampton. (George Greenwell, *Daily Mirror*).

(Above). A welcome brew for rescue workers at Deptford. June 1944. (*Mirrorpix*).

(Above left). A nurse picks through the debris at the Royal Free Hospital, London, following a V1 strike on 30 June 1944. (George Greenwell, *Daily Mirror*).

(Left). Rescuers battle to free Mrs Elsie Smith from the ruins of her home in Whitta Road, East London, following a V1 attack on 24 July 1944. (George Greenwell, *Daily Mirror*).

Mrs Rayner and daughter Susan outside the Anderson shelter they were in when a V1 landed nearby. (*Daily Mirror*).

The house is wrecked, and the only place left to have a wash is out on the street. St Mary's Road, Edmonton. (*Mirrorpix*).

The V1 attacks resulted in a fresh wave of evacuations and not just from London. This image shows evacuees leaving Southampton. Of the 144 V1 rockets that reached England on 15 June, seventy-three are recorded as hitting London, and fifty-three as coming down in the Portsmouth/Southampton area. (*Daily Mirror*).

This London family adopted one of the more unusual ways of avoiding the flying bombs by taking to the up residence in a gypsy caravan in the countryside. (*Mirrorpix*).

The first V2 attack on 8 September 1944. The missile landed on Staveley Road, Chiswick, making a crater 30 ft (9.144 metres) diameter and 8 ft (2.44 metres) deep. Three people were killed and seventeen seriously injured. (George Greenwell, *Daily Mirror*).

Sixty houses were destroyed, and 900 people made homeless when a V2 landed on Tewkesbury Road, Seven Sisters, on 20 January 1945. (George Greenwell, *Daily Mirror*).

Daily Mirror

(MAY 8)

Tuesday, May 8, 1945
No. 12,911 ONE PENNY
Registered at G.P.O. as a Newspaper.

VE-DAY

IT'S OVER IN EUROPE

3 p.m. ANNOUNCEMENT WILL CLINCH IT

TODAY is VE-Day—the day for which British people have fought and endured years, eight months and four days of war.

With unconditional surrender of Germany all the Allies, the war in Europe is over exc for the actions of fanatical Nazis in isola pockets, such as Prague.

The Prime Minister will make an offi announcement—in accordance with arran ments between Britain, Russia and the U.S at three o'clock this afternoon.

ALL TODAY AND TOMORROW ARE PUBLIC HOLID IN BRITAIN, IN CELEBRATION OF OUR VICTORY.

We also remember and salute with gratitude and p the men and women who suffered and died to m triumph possible—and the men still battling in the against another cruel enemy who is still in the field.

WAR WINNERS ON AIR TODA

YOU will hear the voices of the King, Field-Marshals Montgomery and Alexander and General Eisenhower on the B.B.C. Home service tonight.

After the King's speech at 9 p.m. and separated from it by the news bulletin, comes "Victory Report," a special programme which will contain the recorded voices of Ike and Monty, and other famous personalities of war.

This afternoon Mr. Chur announces the end of the w the House of Commons then, at 3 p.m., broadcast the world.

There will be no speec no ceremony in the Ho The Prime Minister will the official document, the once ask that the House journ to St. Marga Chapel for a service thanksgiving.

A procession will the formed, headed by the Spea and all members of the Cabi and will pass through Pa Yard and across Westmins square to the chapel.

Holiday for M.P.s

There will be no furthe ting of the House that M.P.s will meet again tomor Additional features of B.B.C. Home programme, w will end at 2 a.m. tomorrow, clude, at 8 p.m., an address the Archbishop of Canter at a Thanksgiving Service Victory, and at 8.30. "Tri to the King," in which fift people will take part.

They include representat of the Dominions and Colon the three fighting Services Merchant Navy, the Police Civil Defence forces, a flu and a London housewife.

VE-SCENE
TRAFALGAR SQUARE

It was a high old time in Trafalgar-square last night. Everybody wanted to climb something. This party of Wrens and Allied soldiers celebrated by clambering on to the lions. Army policemen present—like Nelson on his column—turned a blind eye.

London's first V-hour

"Daily Mirror" Reporter

PICCADILLY CIRCUS, VE-DAY.

THERE are 10,000 of us here —at a conservative police estimate—in the first hour of this day of days to usher in VE with all the noise that 10,000 people can make when they are out to celebrate.

We had been waiting since two o'clock yesterday for this. We went home at six when it seemed that the news of VE-Day would never come—but we were back in strength for the first minute of VE-Day.

And for some time now we have been making the most of it.

We are dancing the Conga and the jig and "Knees up, Mother Brown," and we are singing and whistling, and blowing paper trumpets.

The idea is to make a noise. We are. Even above the roar of the motors of low-flying bombers "shooting up" the city.

We are dancing around Eros in the black-out, but there is a glow from a bonfire up Shaftesbury-avenue and a news reel cinema has lit its canopy lights for the first time in getting on for six years.

A huge V sign glares down over Leicester Square. And gangs of girls and soldiers of all the Allied nations are waving rattles and shouting and climbing lamp-posts and swarming over cars that have become bogged down in this struggling, swirling mass of celebrating Londoners.

A paper-hatted throng is trying to pull me out of this telephone box now. I hold the door tight, but the din from Piccadilly Circus is drowning my voice.

A group of men liberated from German prison camps are yelling—"Roll out the Barrel."

"We sang it when we went to France in 1939 and we sang it as we tried to get out in 1940," they told me. "Now we sing it for victory."

Amid terrific cheers a New Zealand sailor climbed on the bonnet of a bus and from there to the roof.

He stood there swaying above the crowds as the American army swarmed up after him, but the police fought through the crowd and pulled them down.

Traffic tried to push through

Continued on Back Page

SURRENDER IN A FARMHOUSE

A Reuter message from Rheims described how the surrender was signed at the little red farmhouse which is General Eisenhower's headquarters at 2.41 a.m.

General Jodl, new German Army C.-in-C., signed for Germany.

Victory & Beyond

One of the first signs that normality might be about to return was the lifting of the blackout regulations on 23 April 1945, as what was left of the Luftwaffe in the West was no longer capable of mounting bombing raids on the UK.

One week later, as Soviet troops closed in on the Fuhrerbunker in Berlin, Adolf Hitler and his wife committed suicide and their bodies were burnt in the garden of the Reich Chancellery. Hitler's successor, Admiral Karl Donitz, authorized the military surrender of German forces, signed at SHAEF HQ, Rheims, at 0241hrs on Monday 7 May. The formal unconditional surrender was signed at Karlshorst, Berlin, at 2120 hrs local time on Tuesday 8 May.

Though VE Day marked the ending of the war in Europe, there was still fighting in parts of eastern Europe. The war rumbled on in much of Yugoslavia until 11 May and for two days after that in Czechoslovakia. In Yugoslavia, Tito's Partisans executed around 30,000 Germans, Chetniks and fellow Yugoslavs who had chosen the wrong side. The Western Allies went on to betray the surrendered White Russian and Cossack forces who had fought for Germany. Despite assurances they would be allowed to settle in the West, they were handed over to the USSR and thousands were summarily executed. Within two years of the war ending, estimates as to the number of people who died from war-related problems range from two, to five million.

On 23 May, Prime Minister Winston Churchill resigned, forming a caretaker government until Parliament was dissolved on 15 June. Churchill dominated the Conservative campaign in the country's first general election since 1935, and though he had proved himself an excellent, if at times ruthless wartime leader, he now proved something of a liability when during his first election broadcast, he claimed an incoming Labour administration might form a British equivalent of the Gestapo.

Time for five minutes of fun in snow-swept St Mary Street, Cardiff. January 1945. (*Western Mail & Echo*).

The election was held on 5 July, though counting did not commence until 26 July to allow time for votes cast overseas to reach the UK. Labour won the election on a 9.7 per cent swing, taking 47.7 per cent of the popular vote, giving them 393 seats to the Tories 197. Churchill went to Buckingham Palace to tender his resignation in a chauffeur-driven Rolls-Royce, and incoming Prime Minister Clement Atlee turned up in a Standard Ten driven by his wife.

With the surrender of Japan in August 1945, those who expected life in the UK to quickly return to pre-war conditions were in for a surprise. The US Government immediately pulled the plug on Lend-Lease hurling Britain's new Labour Government into crisis. The country was skint, the war had cost us £7.5 billion (about £330 billion in 2020). Of this vast amount, overseas debt was about £3.3 billion, most of it owed to the United States. Austerity measures would have to remain in force for the foreseeable future.

For those men leaving the armed forces at the beginning of 1945 the clothing ration stood at 48 coupons. A man's suit of utility cloth took 24 coupons and soldiers being discharged early on medical grounds could make a small fortune selling their demob suit. The outfit on Civvy Street would have cost around £12 (£529.60p in 2020) and included a shirt, two collars, a tie, two pairs of socks, a pair of shoes, a raincoat, and a felt hat. The army valued the whole lot at £11 (£485.51p in 2020) though the price could be upped as the buyer stood to save 56 coupons.

The war had changed many. Servicemen who had been out of the country since before the rationing and bombing began, often failed to grasp just what their wives and children had endured. Besides, many women had become independent, competently holding down jobs previously the preserve of men. It came as a shock, when without warning, they were told not to bother coming back the following day as their jobs were being given to men returned from the war.

For others, the man re-entering their life was a stranger, operating to a different set of rules and expectations. Relationships had to begin all over

Getting coal home along a slushy Caledonian Road, London, in January 1945. (*Mirrorpix*).

again. It took toddlers and young children anything up to a year to begin to call the stranger in the room daddy. Many couples failed to adjust to one another and split up.

Then there were the men and women for whom the last six years had been a thrill a minute. They had enjoyed their war and settling back into what passed for normality was a non-starter. One winner of the VC spent 1945-48 smuggling gold sovereigns and gun running around the eastern Mediterranean. A few never bothered returning to the UK. They abandoned their families, sometimes taking on new identities so they could not be traced and started their lives afresh. The number of divorces rose from 8770 in 1939 to 27,789 in 1945.

Others still had jobs to do before they returned to civilian life, such as Romanian-born SOE operative Vera-May Rosenburg. She joined the war crimes division of the Judge Advocate General's Department and was tasked with tracking down and establishing the fates of 117 members of the SOE reported missing presumed dead.

For others there was to be no going home. There was no immediate demobilisation of the Free Polish Armed Forces in the West. Some units were deployed with the occupation forces in the newly created West Germany, others were stationed around the UK. There has been much debate that the Poles were not invited to take part in the 1946 Victory Parade. The British Government ignored the Free Polish forces, inviting instead representatives of the new Communist regime in Warsaw. They never arrived. After a campaign by the Press, the Government invited Polish airmen serving with the RAF, but they turned the offer down when they discovered that the Polish Army and Navy had been ignored. The Polish forces were not disbanded until 1947. Many veterans chose to remain in the UK, others emigrated. Few returned to Poland as the Communist regime had branded them "Enemies of the state," and rumours of imprisonments and executions were filtering back the Polish Government in Exile in London.

During 1946 an estimated 60,000 war brides left the UK bound for their husbands in the USA and Canada. For around 6000 of them life across the

Wrens, sailors, and soldiers celebrate VE Day in Brighton. (Hawkins, *Daily Mirror*).

pond turned out not to be what they had dreamed it would be and they were soon on their way back home. Between 1946 and 1949, more than one million men and women took the opportunity to start afresh and emigrated, with Australia, New Zealand, and Canada the most popular. The Australian Government encouraged immigration with their £10 per person passages.

On 27 June 1946, the government overreacted to a temporary fall in supplies of grain by doing something that had not been done even during the darkest days of the war. Bread was to be rationed from 21 July. The announcement was greeted in the Commons with tense silence. Winston Churchill described it as "one of the gravest I have ever heard in peacetime."

The adult ration was set at nine ounces (255 grams) of bread or flour a day, when at the time a whole loaf was usually fourteen ounces (397 grams), and more than many people already ate. There was an additional ration of up to fifteen ounces (425 grams) for male manual workers. Expectant mothers and women manual workers would get 11 ounces (312 grams), whilst at the other end of the scale, children under one year would get two ounces (57 grams). Bread rationing lasted until 1948.

Within a few years of taking office, Labour had nationalised the railways, coal mines, utilities, airlines, and other key industries. On 5 July 1948, what is probably Labour's crowning glory came into being – the National Health Service offering treatment based upon need and not the ability to pay. Minister of Health Aneurin Bevan stated that in its first full year the NHS would cost the country £249 million (£8.9 billion in 2020). Within twelve months the NHS had issued more than 200 million prescriptions, 4.5 million pairs of spectacles, and 8.5 million people had received free dental care. A concession to consultants was made that they could treat fee-paying clients in NHS hospitals rather than in private consulting rooms.

VE Day at Buckingham Palace. King George VI waves to the tens of thousands of people who had gathered in front of the palace. Also on the balcony are Princess Elizabeth, Queen Elizabeth, and Princess Margaret. They were later joined by Winston Churchill. (Nixon & Greaves, *Daily Herald*).

Housing was another post-war problem. Nationwide only 200,000 new houses were completed during the war years, whilst by early 1946 more than 700,000 were still awaiting repair or demolition. The Housing Act, 1944, provided £150 million (£6.8 billion in 2020) to construct 250,000 homes on a temporary housing programme. The prefab was born. They were bolt together single storey homes that cost £40 (£1814 in 2020) each more than a more traditional brick-built bungalow, but they did come complete with fixtures fittings far beyond what many inner-city dwellers were used to such as flush toilets, fitted kitchens, wash boilers providing a constant supply of hot water. They even had a bit of garden. Desperate families took to squatting in abandoned military installations. Others were able to rent, such as the Nissen huts at Birch Hall Lane, Manchester, where rents ranged between 8s.3d (41p) and 11s.3d (56p) a week though the properties shared one cold water tap and there was no sanitation.

Then on 28 August 1947, newspapers were reporting that the country was going back to a war footing with the introduction of super austerity. The main points were the banning of foreign holidays from 1 October, the meat ration was to be reduced from 1s 2d (6p) to one shilling (5p) from 7 September, and the basic petrol ration was to be abolished. Anyone staying in a hotel would now be required to surrender their ration book after two nights instead of the previous four nights, and hotels and restaurants would face a cut in food supplies of between fifteen and eighteen per cent. Works' canteens would not be affected, neither would places charging not more than 2s 3d (11p) a head for a meal. On a positive note, the tea ration remained at two ounces, expectant mums were to get an extra pint of milk a day together with extra eggs and an extra half ration of meat. They were also entitled to receive vitamins and concentrated orange juice and had priority for bananas and oranges as and when shipments arrived.

Originally, four VE Day services were to be held amid the ruins of Coventry Cathedral, but the crowds were such that additional ones were arranged. They were taken by the provost (the Very Rev R T Howard), and the Bishop of Coventry (Dr Neville Gorton). The Cathedral remained open all night. (*Coventry Telegraph*)

During July 1948, flour was the first item to come off ration. The following year, sweets came off but due to demand outstripping supply, they were put back on after just four months. On 19 May 1950, it was the turn of canned fruit, jellies, mincemeat, syrup, treacle, and chocolate biscuits. Christmas Day for children came on 5 February 1953, when once more sweets came off, even though sugar imports were still only 54 per cent of pre-war levels. Food rationing finally ended after fourteen years on 4 July 1954, when restrictions on the sale of meat and bacon were lifted. For the first time since 1939 wholesale meat markets opened at midnight instead of 6.00 am. The demand for meat rocketed, resulting in the adoption of intensive rearing, especially for chickens. Production rose from five million in 1954 to 75 million in 1959.

Petrol rationing had finally ended in May 1950. The Tories had been arguing for its lifting for some time; the Government response being the lack of US dollars with which to buy the stuff. However, a deal was struck with Standard Oil and California Texas Oil to pay in sterling and in return the companies would invest in British equipment, including oil tankers built in UK shipyards. During 1951 an estimated 430,000 tons of oil was supplied from the USA under these arrangements. A major problem facing the UK was a lack of modern refining capability though two new refineries were under construction.

And the last item to come off ration? That was coal in July 1958. The National Coal Board had amassed a huge stockpile of quality industrial coal due mainly to a fall in demand from Europe, where they were experiencing a recession.

Many towns and cities held VE Parades. Here, US Army nurses take part in the parade through Birmingham. 8 May 1945. (*Birmingham Post & Mail*).

VE Day, Piccadilly Circus, London. (Illustrations Bureau. *Daily Mirror*).

VE Day, Piccadilly Gardens, Manchester. At Trafford Park, hundreds of workers turned up to clock on only to be told to go home. Many were under the impression that the VE Day national holiday would not begin until after Winston Churchill's scheduled 3.00 pm broadcast on the BBC. (*Manchester Evening News*).

VE Day street party, Heaton Park, Manchester. Streets did their own thing, some deciding to wait until Japan had been defeated. Some celebrated held both a VE and a VJ party. (*Manchester Evening News*).

Merryvale Road, Gloucester, VE Day fancy dress party. To flick, or not to flick? That is the question. Resplendent in gypsy costume made by her grannie Gosling, Miss Susan Joan Prince (aged two and a half), contemplates flicking a freshly harvested bogey. (Courtesy, Susan Prince).

During their retreat, German forces breached Holland's coastal defences allowing the North Sea to flood a large area. With the population close to starvation, Dutch children were evacuated to the UK. This contingent of 37 youngsters are pictured after their arrival at Derby Midland station on 30 May. (*Derby Telegraph*).

Holnicote House was used by Somerset County Council as a home for children fathered by African American troops. Born to local women, the children had been given up for adoption. It is estimated that 20,000 children were fathered by American GIs stationed in the UK. Approximately five per cent of these children were black. Recorded illegitimate births for England and Wales increased from 25,500 in 1939 to 63,000 in 1945. (Chapman, *Daily Mirror*).

Back from the USA. Evacuated as schoolgirls and returning as young women to a country where rationing and austerity would continue into the 1950s. (*Mirrorpix*).

VJ street party in full swing at Heeley Road, Selly Oak. (*Birmingham Post & Mail*).

The Dean of St Albans Abbey the Very Reverend C C Thicknesse, said he could not give thanks to God for a victory won by the atomic bomb and banned the use of the abbey for a civic service of thanksgiving.

"I do not hold a service of thanksgiving in St Albans Abbey because I cannot honestly give thanks to God for an event brought about by an act of wholesale indiscriminate massacre." (*Daily Mirror*).

The WLA provided one of the all-female contingents taking part in the 1946 Victory Parade in London. (*Mirrorpix*).

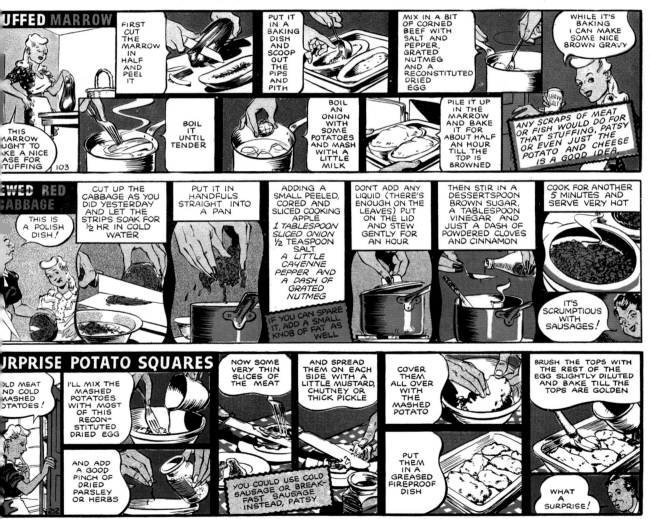

war might be over but rationing continued. The Government issued advice on cooking with limited ingredients
he *Daily Mirror* published Patsy's Cooking Strip. Drawn by Mirror cartoonist Jack Dunkley, each strip was
duced by the paper's gardening columnist Mr Digwell. (*Daily Mirror*).

127

Daily Mirror

THURS JULY 29 1948

ONE PENNY

No. 13,910

Registered at G.P.O. as a Newspaper.

FORWARD WITH THE PEOPLE

NEW BERLIN POLICE CHIEF MOVING H.Q. TO U.S. SECTOR

Dr. Johannes Stumm, Western - appointed police chief of Berlin, said last night police headquarters would be moved from the Russian sector to the American sector on Monday.

According to U.S. Commandant Frank Howley, Paul Markgraf, dismissed Soviet-appointed police chief, meant to have Stumm removed bodily if he took over police H.Q. in the Soviet sector.

Powers agree—back page.

SHOES, CURTAINS OFF THE RATION

Suits, costumes, overcoats and sheets downpointed

"DAILY MIRROR" WOMEN'S CORRESPONDENT

SHOES, furnishing fabrics and curtains, knitted bathing costumes and most children's mackintoshes come off coupons on August 9.

Men's suits will be cut from 26 to 20 coupons. Coupon values of sheets, all women's woollen clothes and boys' shirts will also be reduced by about one-third.

The basic coupon rate for the six months from September 1 stays at four a month.

Announcing these concessions yesterday, Mr. Harold Wilson, President of the Board of Trade, made it clear that his goal is not more coupons, but less clothes rationing.

He estimates that the present concessions,, plus those of last May, give everyone a purchasing power of thirty - six coupons in six months— 50 per cent. above the official ration.

"Prices May Fall"

It textile production doesn't increase to match rising exports, he warned, the basic ration may have to be cut next spring.

But the articles that have been taken off coupons or down-pointed are likely to stay that way.

Some people argue, said Mr. Wilson, that prices are so high that rationing is not necessary, but prices may fall.

"I am not prepared to take risks at this stage with the fair distribution of essential clothing," he added.

Housewives, through their representatives on the committee that advises Mr. Wilson, have won a victory over boys' shirts — raised from four to six in May.

"They convinced me that six coupons is unreasonable high," he said —and shirts are back to their former level

Longer Wait

Supplementary coupons will still be given to children who qualify for them because they need grown-up size clothes.

But they will not be given to children who previously qualified for them because they take extra-large shoes

Men may have to wait longer for their suits, as supplies of worsteds are still short, said Mr. Wilson.

"But," he added, "stocks of women's and children's woollen clothes are good, and I didn't want to discriminate against the men."

Anyone who has ordered a suit and deposited twenty-six coupons, but doesn't get it delivered until after August 9 can ask for six coupons back.

Full list of coupon changes—Page Five.

WORKS BLAST KILL 500, INJURES 250

NEW blasts early today ripped through the IG-Farben chemical works in [ ]wigshaven, in the French Zone of Germany, where between 500 and 600 people died yesterday in an explosion which wrecked a square mile of the city.

About 2,500 people were injured and 100 were still trapped at midnight as flames swept through the miles of buildings along the Rhine bank.

Ghostly Groups

American and French fire-fighting units tried to block the flames as weird, almost ghostly groups of workers covered by a violet dye, still wandered dazed and aimless amid the ruins.

Liquid dyes were scat-

tered over a large are— the explosion, and ma— the other survivors green, yellow, blue or faces.

Scores of workmen reported to have gassed by burning c— cals and air raid s— sounded gas warnings.

The plant is state— have been making plas— unconfirmed reports said that the French been using it to pre— driving fluids for ro— bombs.

DUKE FINDS CL—

Ruby and diamond— found by the Duke of— burgh when he went t— Dorchester last night eve-of-Olympic dinn— was claimed— Lady Inverchapel.

The Olympic Torch sets Kent ablaze on last lap to Wembley

From DONALD ZEC On The Road to Wembley
Thursday morning.

THE Olympic Torch arrived in England last night and set the Kent countryside ablaze with excitement.

From the moment it was on English soil the Torch has led an amazing procession of cars, cyclists,. coaches, motor-cyclists, stretching in the gathering darkness for more than five miles.

The line of twinkling headlights, with the red flame of the Torch in front, tells the story of the trail to Wembley, where the King opens the Olympiad today.

50,000 Cheer

The Flame was landed at Dover last night from the British destroyer Bicester.

It went out a minute after it was handed to Chief Petty Officer Herbert Barnes to carry to the Mayor of Dover.

But it was immediately re-lit from a second Flame brought from Greece in a protective lantern.

Fifty thousand people cheered as Barnes handed the Torch to the Mayor. Councillor A. T. Goodfellow

Anxious Moment

There was an anxious moment when the Mayor raised the flaming Torch Everybody stared apprehensively at his little Van Dyck beard perilously near the Flame.

The Mayor handed the Torch to the second of the seventy-two runners who were to carry it in relays to Wembley—Syd Dobell, a Dover butcher.

Nervously Syd confided to me: "I've been practising for four weeks with a 2½lb. hammer. The muscles of my right arm are twice the size of those on my left."

The Pied Piper

Now we are on the road with a coach behind carrying a spare Torch—and runner. Here is my diary of last night's events:

9 p.m.—Already a two-mile stretch of traffic has been picked up Pied Piper fashion by the runner.

Immediately behind him are hundreds of cyclists. Then a long procession of cars packed two deep and bumper to bumper.

Then coaches, buses, and motor cyclists with huge crowds along the verges.

In the gathering shadows police are fighting to clear road blocks which form at

◆ Continued on Back Page.

The youth of Britain, smiling excitedly, gazing with rapt interest, see Chief Petty Officer Barnes bring the Olympic Torch ashore at Dover.

Time somebody said it, M.P. declares

THE world is sickened of war yet greater war preparations are being made than ever before and people are saying war is inevitable. said Mr. Ellis Smith (Lab., Stoke) in the Commons last night.

"The time has come," he declared, "when a voice should be raised to call a halt."

He spoke of V2's with a 2,500-mile range, of V3's to carry an atomic bomb over a range still secret, of a few atomic bombs making this country uninhabitable.

Mr. W. N. Warbey (Lab., Luton) said we must not tie ourselves to a U.S. military alliance—we must act as a barrier between America and Russia and one day as a bridge.

We were apparently to expect a continual relay of U.S. fighter and bomber

planes visiting this country and occupying our bases.

Was this part of the plan to build up what was now referred to as an Atlantic defence unit?

Mr. C. B. Mayhew, Foreign Under - Secretary, said he did not propose to deal with "the wide and delicate issues" raised by Mr. Ellis Smith and Mr. Warbey.

The foreign affairs debate had been cancelled because it was undesirable to talk about them at the present time

Just after midnight the Speaker said it was difficult for any Government reply to be given because Mr. Bevin was to make a statement today. "We do not want to become a 'talkie-talkie' shop," he said.

When the closure was moved Mr. Blackburn (Lab., King's Norton) tried to raise a point of order that the Speaker had only called speakers critical of the Government.

The Speaker said if he wished to do so he must put down a vote of censure on the chair.

"NO GUNS—NO RUBBER"

Malayan rubber planters have sent the Colonial Office a "No protection— no production" ultimatum. it was reported in Kuala Lumpur yesterday.

GIRL RAN AFTER HOLD-UP MEN

Two men walked into a Post Office in West Green-road, Tottenham, last night and pointed a toy revolver at the two girls behind the counter.

The men tried to climb the grille on the counter but it collapsed. They ran off with £220.

Ethel Stevens, one of the girls, gave chase and warned a police car. Later a man was detained.